MOBILE WEB DESIGN

by CAMERON MOLL

cameromoll

Cameron Moll, Publisher
P.O. Box 1525
Salt Lake City, UT 84110
cameronmoll.com

For updates to this book or to purchase a copy in PDF format, visit mobilewebbook.com.

EDITION
First Edition, Fall 2007

LAYOUT & JACKET DESIGN
Cameron Moll

TYPEFACES
Warnock Pro, designed by Robert Slimbach
Gotham, designed by Tobias Frere-Jones

INSPIRATION
My beautiful wife, Suzanne, whose compassion defies description

ISBN 978-0-6151-8591-0

ACKNOWLEDGMENTS

I couldn't possibly have published this book without the assistance, guidance, and encouragement of many individuals over the course of two years:

Conference organizers who believed in me enough to extend a speaking invite for their events: Brad Smith (Webvisions 2005), Patrick Griffiths (@media 2006), Philipp Hoschka (W3C Mobile Web Seminar 2006).

Brian Fling as the technical editor for the original Mobile Web Design series of articles on my site.

David Storey for providing insight into Opera Mobile and Opera Mini.

Those who provided feedback with the original Markup Test Pages in 2005: Brian Rose, Anthony Cervo, Jan Brasna, Glenda Sims, Kim Siever, Blake Scarbrough, Jamie Dearnley, Shannon Hager, Lode Vermeiren, Paul Haine, Colin Frame, Hayo Bethlehem, Sean Madden, Ricky Moorhouse, David Stutler.

Those who accepted review copies and provided thorough input and corrections: Luca Passani, Andy Moore, Rocco Georgi, Andrea Trasatti, C. Enrique Ortiz, Jo Rabin, Ryan Unger, Ajit Jaokar, Matthew Pennell, John Gruber, Barbara Ballard, Jared Benson, James Pearce, Bronwyn Jones, Tim Zheng, Clifton Labrum.

Talented individuals who brought mobilewebbook.com to life: Jesse Bennett-Chamberlain, Marion Newman, Jonathan Linczak, Myles Grant.

Above all, my wife and four boys for the countless hours they endured while I authored this book.

CONTENTS

INTRODUCTION

THIS IS A BOOK ABOUT DELIVERING web content to mobile devices. Much has been written about mobile devices. Plenty has been written about developing websites for the so-called "standards era" of the web. However, little has been written about the two colliding. This resource aims to fill that void.

The premise of this book is threefold: Analyze current and future technologies relevant to mobile web content, confront the limitations of existing mobile devices, and discover methods for exploiting the unique opportunities afforded by mobility and its devices, both current and future.

I'm a firm believer that the "mobile web"—a phrase used throughout this book to loosely represent "accessing web content on a mobile device"—is the biggest thing since sliced images. More people worldwide have access to a mobile phone than a PC, and that means only one thing: More people to access, manipulate, use, and expend the web content you've worked so hard to create. This was one of the driving forces behind the writing of this book.

IS THIS BOOK FOR YOU?

If you're in a position to develop for, manage, or give advice regarding your organization's foray into—or extended development of—a web strategy for mobile devices, then this book is for you.

This book makes a few key assumptions:

- You have at least a basic understanding of XHTML and CSS
- You know little or nothing about formatting web content for mobile devices
- You or your organization is unsure about, interested in, or possibly affected by the future of this "mobile web thing"

Let's also set some expectations: This is not a highly technical book offering extensive tutorials for creating mobilized websites. Instead, it covers the fundamentals of design and development for mobile devices, the methodology behind developing content for those devices, and offers some tips to get things rolling.

At the end of the day, there are simply too many topics to be afforded by just one book, and therefore I've written *Mobile Web Design* as a starting point for those who qualify themselves according to the three assumptions just mentioned. Supplementary resources may include the following, most of which are available at quality bookstores:

- *Designing the Mobile User Experience* by Barbara Ballard
- *dotMobi Mobile Web Developer's Guide* (available at http://dev.mobi)
- *Global Authoring Practices for the Mobile Web* by Luca Passani (available at http://www.passani.it/gap)
- *Constant Touch: A Global History of the Mobile Phone* by Jon Agar
- *Personal, Portable, Pedestrian: Mobile Phones in Japanese Life* by Mizuko Ito, Daisuke Okabe, and Misa Matsuda
- *Mobile Interaction Design* by Matt Jones and Gary Marsden

While accessing the web on a mobile device is nothing new, a renewed interest in developing mobile web content has been ignited by notable efforts from groups such as W3C's Mobile Web Initiative and dotMobi (among many others), an abundance of skilled XHTML/CSS developers, and the increased availability of more capable devices such as iPhone (Figure 1-1).

Figure 1-1. My site (http://cameronmoll.com) as viewed with an Apple iPhone.

I CAN READ MINDS

I'll let you in on a little secret: I can read minds. I know what you're thinking: "Why should I care about mobile? After all, the mobile web experience isn't nearly as good as the desktop web experience."

You're not alone. That's a mistake many of us traditional "desktop" web developers, managers, and producers make when assessing the mobile web experience. We long for it to be the same as the desktop experience.

The truth of the matter is web content on mobile devices can be every bit as good of an experience, but in its own right. If we treat the mobile web as its own environment rich with possibilities, rather than a crippled extension of the desktop experience with restrictive limitations, we begin to understand how to embrace and even exploit those possibilities.

By now you may have heard the facts: Mobile handset proliferation is expected to increase to 4 billion subscribers worldwide by 2010.[1] Coupled with the U.N. prediction of 6.8 billion humans by 2010, **4 billion mobile subscribers is an astounding 59% of the planet!** Just how many of those subscribers will have data plans and web-enabled phones remains to be seen, but inevitably this all means one thing for you and me: Scores of potential consumers of web content on mobile devices.

Figure 1-2. Left: The New York Times Mobile (http://mobile.nytimes.com) as viewed with a Palm Treo 650 using the native Blazer 4.0 browser. Right: Yahoo Mobile (http://yahoo.mobi) as viewed with a Nokia 6680 using Opera Mini 3.0 browser.

---

[1] Dan Nystedt, "Mobile Subscribers to Reach 2.6B This Year," http://www.pcworld.com/article/id,127820/article.html.

But let's bring things back down to earth for a moment: It's fair to say accessing web content on a mobile device, as it stands today, is a rather inconsistent experience. Several dozen mobile user agents (browsers) exist today, each rendering markup in different ways. The choice to use WML, XHTML Mobile Profile, XHTML Basic, or cHTML can be an overwhelming decision, to say the least. And what about web addresses? Is it mobile.mysite.com, mysite.com/wap, mysitemobile.com, mysite.mobi? Where does device detection and content adaptation fit in?

There is hope! This book is a start. It won't answer all of your questions, but my hope is that it spawns a desire not only to learn more but also to go forth with confidence in producing a successful mobile web endeavor. Consider the following:

> *"Nearly three-quarters of people are avoiding the mobile Internet because of high costs and poor experiences of the technology, according to research published today. **The findings highlight the need for firms to develop mobile-compatible content,** said experts."*[2]

The need for confident designers and developers, willing to discover new and relevant ways to present mobilized data, is significant. The need is now. This is where you come in.

A LEGACY OF MOBILITY

In *Constant Touch: A Global History of the Mobile Phone,* Jon Agar profiles Swedish electrical engineer Lars Magnus Ericsson—a surname undoubtedly recognized by many mobile users. In 1910, retired and "backed by a healthy bank balance" from his successful telegraph and telephone business, Ericsson "built a telephone into his wife Hilda's car, the vehicle connected by wires and

---

[2] Phil Muncaster, "Public Is Shunning the Mobile Web," http://www.itweek.co.uk/itweek/news/2161798/public-shun-mobile-web.

poles to the overhead telephone lines that had sprung up in rural Sweden. Enough power for a telephone could be generated by cranking a handle and, while Ericsson's mobile telephone was in a sense a toy, it did work."

From an isolated experiment in rural Sweden a century ago, to the first bona fide mobile phones in the '70s and '80s, to now nearly 3 billion devices spanning industrialized and non-industrialized countries alike, mobile phone proliferation is nothing short of astounding. In fact, so ubiquitous has the technology become that today more than 20% of Europeans[3] and 15-17% of North Americans[4] have at least two phones—one for business and another for personal use.

Much more than just a toy, mobile phones have weaved their way into the social, cultural, and economic underpinnings of business and personal life. And yet our understanding of these devices and their impact on society is still relatively nascent, as observed by Mizuko Ito et al. in *Personal, Portable, Pedestrian: Mobile Phones in Japanese Life*:

> *"To say only that mobile phones cross boundaries, heighten accessibility, and fragment social life is to see only one side of the dynamic social reconfigurations heralded by mobile communications. Mobile phones create new kinds of bounded places that merge the infrastructures of geography and technology, as well as technosocial practices that merge technical standards and social norms."*

In short, a rich legacy of mobile exploration is likely to yield an even richer future of discovery as we continue to grasp the many ways in which mobile

---

[3] Michael Mace, "European vs. American Mobile Phone Use," http://mobileopportunity.blogspot.com/2006/09/european-vs-american-mobile-phone-use.html.

[4] Alex Moskalyuk, "15-17% of Americans and Canadians Use More Than One Mobile Phone," http://blogs.zdnet.com/ITFacts/?p=11938.

communications *fit* into social life, but also as we uncover the many ways in which they are *shaping* the very core of it.

DEVICE SCREENS SHOWN IN THIS BOOK

I currently operate seven phones on two networks:

- Nokia 6680
- Nokia 6800
- Motorola RAZR V3
- Palm Treo 650
- Sony Ericsson K750i
- Samsung SGH-E630
- Apple iPhone 8GB

The Treo 650 is on the Sprint network, while the other six operate on the AT&T network. I swap a single SIM card between the six AT&T devices.

Figure 1-3. Six phones that I currently operate (left to right): Nokia 6680, Nokia 6800, Motorola RAZR V3, Palm Treo 650, Sony Ericsson K750i, Samsung SGH-E630. Not pictured: Apple iPhone, which was acquired shortly before publication.

Whenever a screen is shown in this book, the device used and a URL for the website or application shown will be mentioned. In some cases, the URL for the mobile site is the same as the desktop site because of device detection, which is discussed later in this book.

The screen images featured in this book are a combination of photos I've taken manually and actual screenshot software. For screenshots, software was downloaded and installed on some devices, which included Screenshots v1.0 on my Nokia 6680 and ScreenShot v2.3 on my Treo 650. For devices on which suitable screenshot software wasn't available, such as the Motorola RAZR, photos of the screen were taken using a Canon PowerShot SD600.

MOBILE WEB FUNDAMENTALS

EVERY SO OFTEN A WEB ARTICLE comes along worthy of a good sit-down read, a print and staple, or a browser bookmark entry. Best-selling author and mobile expert Tomi Ahonen's **Putting 2.7 Billion in Context: Mobile Phone Users** (http://communities-dominate.blogs.com/brands/2007/01/putting_27_bill.html) is not only all of the above, but I'd consider it required reading for anyone considering a foray into mobile content, especially fence-sitters unsure about making the leap. Ahonen's lengthy but discerning article compares mobile phone penetration to that of the car, the telephone, the TV, and other forms of ubiquitous technology.

2.7 BILLION MOBILE USERS IN CONTEXT

The thrust of Ahonen's article is comparing common technologies used in everyday life in many parts of the world, the number of years available to consumers, and worldwide usage (Figure 2-1).

Consider the implications: In just 35 years—roughly the same amount of time as the PC and nearly one-fourth that of the landline phone—mobile phone penetration has surpassed the PC and landline phone *combined,* reaching 2.7 billion mobile subscriptions in 2006.[1] In fact, in some of the more developed

---

[1] Chetan Sharma, "Global Wireless Data Market Update 2006", http://www.chetansharma.com/worlddatatrends2006.htm.

areas of the world, penetration is at 100% or better.[2] In 2006, Western Europe crossed the 100% wireless subscriber penetration mark with some nations such as Italy reporting up to 140% subscriber penetration. Astoundingly, this literally means there are more mobiles than humans in these countries. Comparatively, the U.S. achieved 75% penetration in 2006. (Statistics for nearly every country in the world can be found at http://mobileactive.org/countries.)

TYPE	YEARS	WORLD USAGE
Automobile	100	800 million
PC	30	850 million
Landline Phone	110	1.3 billion
Credit Card	40	1.4 billion
TV	60	1.5 billion
Mobile Phone	**35**	**2.7 billion**

Figure 2-1. Common technologies used in everyday life. (Rough estimates are provided only for the sake of comparison.)

Tomi Ahonen further illustrates the importance of mobile penetration by explaining that regions such as Africa are:

> *"... in a hurry to increase phone penetration after the OECD study found that increasing mobile phone penetration results in the greatest benefit to the GDP of an emerging country. Better benefit than providing computers, electricity, roads etc. You don't need a literate population to have benefits from phones, but you do need literacy for personal computers."*

---

[2] Penetration is usually measured using mobile subscriber data for age 15 and older, and the final count may include subscribers with multiple SIM cards.

It's difficult to overstate the worldwide ubiquity of the mobile phenomenon, if merely for the fact that subscription growth is rampant in what seems to be the most unexpected places. Consider India, which has surpassed China to become the fastest-growing cellular market in the world, adding more than 5 million subscribers monthly towards the latter part of 2006.[3] China, however, seems to be in a league of its own, recently adding its 301-millioneth subscriber, a number which exceeds the entire U.S. population. Granted, ubiquity in behemoth China might not be unexpected, but how about Kenya, where the number of mobiles has grown from one million to 6.5 million in the last five years, while the number of landlines remains at about 300,000.[4]

Given this is a book about the mobile web, the question then becomes how many of these worldwide subscribers are accessing the web from their mobile devices? According to a study conducted in January 2007 by Telephia and comScore, two leading research firms for mobile media and internet metrics respectively, **5.7 million people in the U.K.** used a mobile device to access the web compared to 30 million who accessed the web from a PC. **In the U.S., 30 million** of the 176 million web users accessed the mobile web. The most popular sites in the U.K. included BBC, MSN-Windows Live, Yahoo!, Google, and SKY, whereas in the U.S. the most popular sites were Yahoo!, MSN-Windows Live, Google, The Weather Channel, and AOL.[5]

Do the math on these numbers and mobile web usage in the U.S. and U.K. is **between 17 and 19 percent of PC web usage.** In other words, the mobile web audience is already one-fifth the size of the PC web audience in some areas of

---

[3] Saritha Rai, "Mobile Phone Proliferates, A Hallmark Of New India," The New York Times, http://mobilewebbook.com/shorty/15990.

[4] Paul Mason, "From Matatu to the Masai Via Mobile," BBC News, http://news.bbc.co.uk/2/hi/technology/6241603.stm.

[5] comScore Press Release, "Mobile Web Audience Already One-Fifth the Size of PC-Based Internet Audience in the U.K.," May 14, 2007, http://www.comscore.com/press/release.asp?press=1432.

the world. So, is there traction behind this mobile web thing? I'd say the numbers speak for themselves.

COMMUNICATING WITHIN AN ENVIRONMENT OF MOBILITY

Lest we get carried away with stats and tables, let's step back for a minute and look at the underlying concepts of the phrase "mobile design."

The first element of this two-part phrase is *mobile*. I adore Barbara Ballard's definition, included in her latest book, *Designing the Mobile User Experience*:

> *"Fundamentally, 'mobile' refers to the user, and not the device or the application."*

Mobile, the user; not mobile, the device. Mobile is more than just being wireless. Mobility transcends freedom from wires; it suggests an entirely different user experience. For example, a wireless router enables me to roam from room to room within my house or to connect to the web at a local Starbucks. I'm using the same laptop in each case. What's more, I'm probably accessing data in much the same format I do from my desktop computer.

In contrast, a mobile device, say my Nokia 6680 phone, requires an entirely different user experience. The device is smaller. The screen is miniscule in comparison to most modern desktop displays. Input methods are often much different than that of a QWERTY keyboard. Further, I might be accessing that data while holding a bottle of water or while gripping a handle on the subway. I might be seeking only contextual data such as directions or a contact's number, rather than the plethora of data at my disposal via a desktop PC. And in many cases, I want to do things with my mobile that I just can't do with my PC.

In short, comprehending the experience of consuming, manipulating, and reporting data, and the context in which that experience occurs, is imperative to the creator of the data.

The second element is *design,* a medium through which a message is conveyed and response is sought. Design is certainly first and foremost communication, yet what separates design from other forms of communication, such as speech and the written word, is that it cannot exist without a medium—print, multimedia, signage, canvas, and so on. Further, what separates design from art is that design "is meant to be … functional."[6] In a practical sense, design attempts to acquire a response from the viewer or to facilitate an experience.

Therefore, based on the elaborate definitions just provided, the phrase "mobile design" really means *the discipline of communicating within an environment of mobility.* When planning a mobile web strategy, this deeper understanding yields **context** (e.g. "Jill Smith is on the go"), **user experience** (e.g. "Jill typically consumes and sends content using only one hand"), and **focus** (e.g. "How can we serve Jill's needs on the go, while requiring minimal dexterity?").

CONFRONTING LIMITATIONS, EXPLOITING OPPORTUNITIES

If this book had a mantra, it might be something akin to the heading for this section: "Confront limitations. Exploit opportunities." It's fair to state firstly that there is certainly no shortage of limitations currently facing mobile web developers and users. Small screen size is the most obvious challenge. Difficulty of data input is another shortcoming cited frequently. User agent (browser) inconsistency, not only the usability of the interface from agent to agent but markup rendering as well, is no small chore to deal with as a developer.

But what of the opportunities unique to mobile, especially those unattainable within the desktop web environment? Location-specific data, on-the-go messaging, and of course handheld voice communication are just a few. When you consider the mobile phone as a portable device that can service voice calls,

---

[6] Linda Tischler, "The Future of Design," Fast Company, July/August 2006.

access web content, and store and retrieve data on the go, you begin to realize it's an incredibly efficient tool for managing data within an environment of mobility.

Gaddo F. Benedetti, in his article for dev.mobi (dotMobi's developer portal), elaborates on the need to exploit mobile:

> "[W]hat sells the mobile Web is not how it is similar to the desktop Web, but how it differs. The mobile Web is a phenomenal platform to build and exploit applications. But until even we, the industry who build them, stop thinking of it as primarily 'the Internet on your phone,' both users and clients will see it as little more than a poor man's browser, making it a far harder ROI to sell to potential clients."[7]

Figure 2-2. The Weather Channel (http://weather.mobi) as viewed with a Nokia 6680 using the native Symbian OS browser.

The Weather Channel gets it. They've managed to exploit mobile to the extent that in the U.S. the Weather Channel has a greater reach via the mobile web (Figure 2-2) than it does via the PC-based web.[8]

It's in your best interest, and the interest of your users, to find ways to capitalize on the unique opportunities of mobile, much like the Weather Channel, while still confronting existing limitations. I'll be the first to admit these limitations present a formidable challenge for developers. However, these limitations most certainly won't subsist

---

[7] Gaddo F. Benedetti, "Mobile First, Web Second," http://dev.mobi/node/156.

[8] comScore Press Release, "Mobile Web Audience Already One-Fifth the Size of PC-Based Internet Audience in the U.K.," May 14, 2007, http://www.comscore.com/press/release.asp?press=1432.

indefinitely. For example, someday we may be using foldable or rollable displays that serve the best of both worlds: mobility and readability. In fact, the **Readius by Polymer Vision** (Figure 2-3) proves rollable displays are already slated for the not-so-distant future.

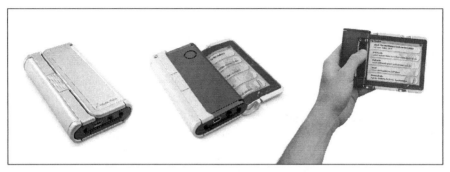

Figure 2-3. Polymer Vision Readius, a rollable display prototype. See a demo of the Readius at http://youtube.com/watch?v=uQMBzXaCmqY. (Images copyright Polymer Vision. Used by permission.)

User agent inconsistency is another challenge that must be confronted, but also one that will improve over time. While estimates vary considerably, it's safe to assume there are more than a few hundred web-ready mobile devices on the market and a few dozen types of user agents installed on those devices. This presents a considerable challenge for developers, as testing on, let alone access to, the range of devices a given target audience may use is often costly and impractical. So in the short-term, nothing short of emulators and testing on multiple devices will lead to the successful deployment of a website or application.

In the near future, however, improvements in consistency will likely occur. **Opera Mini** (Figure 2-4), developed by Opera Software and already in version 4.x, is blazing a trail that aims to provide greater consistency across devices.

Figure 2-4. Opera Mini browser (start page).

Note the subtle rendering differences between the Symbian OS browser and Opera Mini shown in Figure 2-5—the select menu is trimmed to reduce wrapping, unnecessary whitespace is eliminated to provide more room for content, and image size is reduced to minimize data download.

Available as a free download at http://operamini.com, Opera Mini serves as a replacement to your device's native browser, and it's compatible with many phones on the market today. It levels the playing field for developers, and more importantly, it provides better consistency for users as they switch phones or carry multiple devices. The flow of the user interface is also far more optimal than most native browsers.

Figure 2-5. Rendering differences between Symbian OS browser (left) and Opera Mini (right).

Regrettably, third-party software such as Opera Mini must be installed by the device owner, and rarely ever does anyone upgrade the browser software on their phone. However, T-Mobile has been shipping hundreds of thousands of its handsets with Opera Mini pre-installed[9], Mozilla is considering a mobile version of Firefox[10], and the browser in Apple's iPhone is essentially Safari "Mini". All things considered, browsers on the horizon will undoubtedly provide increased consistency for users and developers alike.

CONTEXT IS KING

The importance of comprehending context—circumstances and conditions that surround a place, thing, or event—within the mobile environment cannot be overstated. Your content is of little value to users if it ignores the context in which it is viewed, manipulated, and processed. Consider how you access content on your mobile device. You're on the subway (or tube), or you're walking to your next appointment. You're holding your handset in one hand, coffee in the other. You're glancing up to prevent a run-in with a pole or to be sure you haven't missed your stop.

The mobile web is very much a context-, content-, and component-sensitive environment. Or put another way, access to web content on a mobile device is largely influenced by surrounding conditions (context), informational relevance to the task at hand (content), and the feature capabilities of the device being used (components). Unlike the desktop web experience, where screen space is liberal, web access is fast and reliable, and data input is facilitated by keyboard and mouse, the mobile web experience is often a small screen, intermittent, one-handed experience.

Misunderstanding the importance of context may be akin to the thinking behind the product shown in Figure 2-6. It's clear that whoever designed this product isn't a cat owner. Few owners would place a litter box next to the living room couch for all family members and friends to enjoy the odors

---

[9] BetaNews, "T-Mobile to Offer Opera Mini in Europe," http://www.betanews.com/article/ TMobile_to_Offer_Opera_Mini_in_Europe/1141840092.

[10] Dan Warne, "Firefox Will Move to Mobile Phones: Mozilla CEO," http://apcmag.com/6041/ firefox_will_move_to_mobile_phones_mozilla_ceo.

emitted therefrom. So while the underlying idea—hiding a litter box inside a usable planter pot—has merit, the product's resulting placement entirely ignores the context in which it's used.

Figure 2-6. *Advertisement for a decorative litter box.*

And so it is with mobile. Your big idea will ultimately be of little value if it ignores the context in which users interact with your big idea. Any mobile web strategy must begin with an understanding of the target audience and what they want from a site or app, and what the contextual relevance of such a site or app is. Ask yourself, what is relevant to my users and the tasks, problems, and needs they may encounter while being mobile? Begin by answering that question, and you're guaranteed to start on the right foot.

A simple example of contextual relevance is the University of Texas (UT) mobilized directory (Figure 2-7). While the aesthetics aren't terribly attractive, the utility is.

In addition to typical directory data such as name, phone number, and location, the directory's search results are contextual in at least two ways.[11]

---

[11] Neither of these methods are supported by all phones on the market today, so use these methods only after adequate testing on phone models used by your target audience.

First, the phone number is linked using code that invokes a phone call:

```
Office: <a href="wtai://wp/mc;+15554755138">1 555 475 5138</a>
```

The reference wtai://wp/mc; instructs the handset to place a call using the phone number value that follows the semicolon. Be aware that the WTAI (Wireless Telephony Application Interface) protocol is traditionally associated with WML. The recommended alternative for doing the same with XHTML markup is the tel: protocol:

```
Office: <a href="tel:+15554755138">1 555 475 5138</a>
```

Some browsers, such as Opera Mini and Safari on iPhone, will convert phone numbers into links automatically, even in the absence of tel: markup.

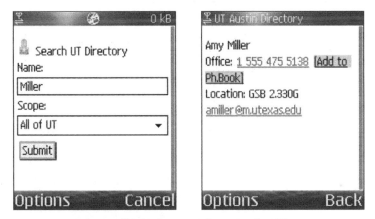

Figure 2-7. University of Texas directory information (http://mobile.utexas.edu) as viewed with a Nokia 6680 using the native browser. (Personal data has been changed.)

Second, a user can conveniently add a person to his or her address book merely by clicking a link:

```
<a href="wtai://wp/ap;+15554755138;Amy%20Miller">
    [Add to Ph.Book]</a>
```

The reference `wtai://wp/ap;` instructs the handset to add the contact name and phone number using the device's default address book application. Currently, a recommended alternative to do the same with XHTML does not exist, but this could very well be facilitated by microformats in the future **when, not if,** mobile browsers offer support for microformats.[12]

For additional reading on the importance of context, see **The Mobile Context** (http://weblog.cenriqueortiz.com/mobile-context) by C. Enrique Ortiz.

OVERCOMING CARRIER MYOPIA

Let's cut to the chase: Some seasoned mobile developers suffer from carrier (operator) myopia. That is to say, they believe carriers (e.g. Vodafone, Orange, AT&T, Verizon, etc.) have, and will continue to have, complete control over the availability of web content through their networks. Traditionally this has been the case, as most users had restricted access only to websites approved by the operator or carrier, often referred to as a carrier deck, closed portal, or walled garden (Figure 2-8).

To their credit, carriers have done much to fuel the growth of mobile subscriptions by subsidizing the cost of phones, managing the complex infrastructure of wireless networks, and lots more. They're entitled to profit from it all. But as Time Magazine contributor Jeremy Caplan puts it, "Imagine if Seinfeld were available only on RCA televisions. Or if your broadband service let you use Hotmail but not Gmail. That's not far from the state of the mobile phone system today. The carriers rule."[13]

---

[12] Microformats are an easy way to classify and share data by inserting simple classes and IDs in the markup for information such as people and organizations, calendars and events, and the like. Using these standardized open formats, data can then be shared among other sites and applications. Learn more at http://microformats.org.

[13] Jeremy Caplan, "The iPhone Kick-Starts the Competition," Time Magzine, July 2, 2007, p. 36.

I know first-hand that this myopia exists as I've worked with several seasoned mobile developers who, at the onset of our relationship and with good intentions, adamantly tried to convince me the only way to provide mobile web content to users was by landing a spot on the carrier deck. I don't believe that's the case now, and I certainly don't believe that will be the case moving forward.

Figure 2-8. AT&T carrier deck (formerly referred to as MEdia Net) as viewed with a Motorola RAZR using the native browser.

The Mobile User Experience (MEX) Conference, a strategy forum for the mobile telecom industry, released a manifesto prior to its 2007 conference. The manifesto's second point speaks of overcoming carrier myopia:

> *"Tearing down the walled garden will enhance the mobile content experience and release value for the industry. The objective should be a free market for content and applications, based on open standards and accessible to all. We think the current fragmentation of formats and channels to market is holding back growth."*

Amen. With the rapid exchange of data from one web user to another in today's economy, an "open garden" wherein users have unrestricted access to content will be critical to fueling mobile web growth and facilitating the sharing of information, irrespective of carrier choice. In the words of wireless industry analyst Dean Bubley, "choice of service provider is irrelevant when you tell your friends to 'check this out!'"[14]

AVOIDING PC NEARSIGHTEDNESS

Perhaps the most common blunder committed by newcomers to mobile development is to replicate the PC web experience. This blunder might be referred to as "PC nearsightedness", wherein a developer's interpretation of web content is limited to that which is most familiar and closest within view: The desktop PC.

Esteemed author Barbara Ballard confronts this issue in her article, **Mobilize, Don't Miniaturize** (http://www.littlespringsdesign.com/design/mobilize). **Miniaturizing** "treats the mobile environment and technology as a subset of the desktop environment." It fails to consider the strengths and weaknesses of mobile devices. **Mobilizing,** on the other hand, "precisely targets mobile user needs, making [the] best possible use of technology." Contextual user tasks, not the existing website, determine the content, architecture, and user experience of the mobilized site.

The root of the problem behind PC nearsightedness lies in the fact that many of us in industrialized countries don't know the web any other way than via PC. This was best expressed by a reader who replied to a discussion on my site, "The new [iPhone] browser allows webpages to be viewed 'like they are meant to be.'" This opinion exemplifies the miniaturization mindset—that sites are viewed "correctly" on the desktop, and that they should then be viewed the same on alternate devices. What if the web had hit mobiles first before desktop machines back in the early '90s? That might sound foolish, but truth of the matter is it's happening today with some regions of the world, where access to

---

[14] Dean Bubley, "3GSM: Mobile Content is Officially Dead. Long Live the Real Internet on Mobiles," http://disruptivewireless.blogspot.com/2007/02/3gsm-mobile-content-is-officially-dead.html.

the web is done first—and sometimes exclusively—via mobile device. Consider this forecast by Tomi Ahonen:

> *"During 2007 the first cross-over will happen, with more users accessing [the internet] via phone than PC. Fascinating data coming on that usage as well, the Japanese regulator reports that those who access the web via mobile phone do so more frequently than those who access via a PC."*[15]

An immediate, LASIK-like correction of PC nearsightedness can be brought about by asking yourself two questions: If users frequented a mobile version of my site more often than a PC version, what content would be of value to them? If they accessed the mobile version exclusively, what would the experience be like?

"CELL PHONE" IS SO DYNATAC

If you're a U.S. citizen, listen up: You must rid your vocabulary of the term "cell phone." We're one of the few economies on the planet to refer to a mobile phone in that way.[16] If you care to find yourself in any of the worthwhile mobile development circles, begin using terms more widely accepted: "mobile," "mobile phone," "handset," "handy," or even just "device." If you're not sure which, go for "mobile." Such as, "Yo dog, check out my new mobile."

---

[15] Tomi Ahonen, "Putting 2.7 billion in Context: Mobile Phone Users," http://communities-dominate.blogs.com/brands/2007/01/putting_27_bill.html.

[16] As Jon Agar recounts in *Constant Touch: A Global History of the Mobile Phone*, the term "cell phone" traces its roots in the U.S. as far back as 1947, when a Bell Labs engineer by the name of D.H. Ring proposed a pattern of hexagonal, adjacent "cells" that, in theory, would provide uninterrupted coverage for phones that operated by radio (an idea which remained unpublished for nearly 20 years).

If you're in Japan, on the other hand, the term you'd use is "keitai," a label whose meaning extends beyond infrastructure and mobility:

> *"In contrast to the cellular phone of the United States (defined by technical infrastructure), and the mobile of the United Kingdom (defined by the untethering from fixed location) (Kotamraju and Wakeford 2002), the Japanese term keitai (roughly translated, 'something you carry with you') references a somewhat different set of dimensions. A keitai is not so much about a new technical capability or freedom of motion but about a snug and intimate technosocial tethering, a personal device supporting communications that are a constant, lightweight, and mundane presence in everyday life."[17]*

Whatever the term, I implore you to start calling that little device you carry with you something other than "cell phone."

---

[17] Mizuko Ito et al., *Personal, Portable, Pedestrian: Mobile Phones in Japanese Life,* (MIT Press, 2005).

FOUR METHODS, REVISITED

IN FALL 2005, FOLLOWING A SUMMER spent doing research and conference speaking related to the mobile web, I packaged my findings into a series of articles and published them under the label, **Mobile Web Design: The Series** (http://www.cameronmoll.com/archives/000398.html). The second article in the series offered four methods for strategizing and deploying mobile web content (Figure 3-1).

Figure 3-1. The second article in the Mobile Web Design series, "Methods to the Madness," was published in August 2005.

When I first authored these methods, the industry climate was somewhat overcast—no one really knew where the mobile web was headed. Two years later (has it been that long?), the air is clearer, and yet these four approaches are still very applicable. Thus, what follows is an updated account of these methods, including a revised look at the advantages and disadvantages of each.

1. DO NOTHING

"Summon the WAP gods and pray the site renders well" was this method's opening line in the original article. While prayer and finger crossing remain necessary largely because of the wide disparity in the way mobile browsers render markup, I echo the argument I made previously—doing nothing special for mobile devices remains a viable approach for at least the following two reasons.

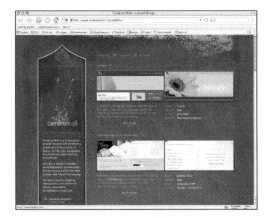

Figure 3-2. The desktop version of http://cameronmoll.com/portfolio (left) and the same version as rendered with Opera Mini (right), with no structural changes to the markup or images.[1]

---

[1] I'd be flattered if users wanted to access my portfolio on their phones, but in all reality it's not something the average user would do. This is yet another example of contextual relevance, wherein better value could be provided by considering which parts of my site users want to access with their mobile device and in what context they'll do so, the result of which may be something akin to http://cameronmoll.com/mobile.

First, if the markup is meaningful and standards-based, some of the better mobile browsers are fairly adept at repurposing sites on the fly to fit the smaller widths of mobile screens. A website isn't merely reduced in size, but rather the layout is linearized and images are optimized to present content more efficiently (Figure 3-2). All content adaptation is done by the browser, relieving the developer of the need to repurpose content specifically for mobile.

Second, devices such as **iPhone** (Figure 3-3) whose browsers are capable of content zooming—the ability to see an entire web page and zoom in or out, also referred to as adaptive zooming or mini-map navigation—make possible the viewing of full-featured websites as seen much the same from a desktop PC. The resulting argument is to leave content alone and do no adaptation for mobile—or better yet, design web content to work across many machines and devices by design—allowing these zoom-enabled browsers to offer users an experience similar to that of the desktop.

Figure 3-3. The Apple iPhone, introduced in 2007. (Image copyright Apple, Inc. Used by permission.)

However, there are certainly disadvantages to this approach. Quite frankly, those who argue mobilized sites should be the same as their desktop counterparts probably haven't accessed the mobile web much, as difficulty of data entry, slow network speeds, and the click/refresh model we're used to on the desktop all too often combine to present a frustrating user experience.

Further, iPhone, Blackberry, and Treo owners aren't necessarily the typical mobile web user. In many cases, these devices comprise only a small portion of global markets. In fact, if the mobile web is to become anything more than rich internet access for elite phone subscribers, we must look beyond Blackberrys, Treos, and yes, iPhones. Recently India has been outpacing all other countries in mobile subscriptions growth, but don't expect them to be mass-market iPhone owners anytime soon—or at least owners of devices with similar capabilities, speaking in terms of a market majority.

Lastly, and most importantly, context is still king. At the end of the day, robust devices such as iPhone are still devices built for mobility. We can safely assume these devices and other devices yet to be produced will be small enough to fit in a pocket, and thus we can probably expect users to endure the small-screen, intermittent, one-handed experience of consuming and reporting content that we've come to know.

Advantages of this method:

- Mobile browsers shoulder the burden of reformatting content
- No additional effort is required on the part of the web development team
- Users have access to the same content, and possibly even the same experience, available from a desktop PC

Disadvantages of this method:

- Doing nothing does nothing to address the contextual relevance of mobility, nor does it exploit the unique capabilities of mobility
- Users with zoom-enabled devices comprise a very small share of the global mobile market, while users with less capable "market majority" devices will likely not have a very compelling content experience

2. REDUCE IMAGES AND STYLING

Recognizing most devices on the market today support HTML in addition to WML (see chapter, **WAP 2.0: An XHTML Environment**), this method relies on the strength and implicit hierarchy of markup to deliver a navigable, content-rich experience. Presentational styling and images are reduced on the fly—either optimized to reduce file size or eliminated entirely—leaving raw, minimally styled content.

Several resources already exist that allow both the user and the developer to perform this raw rendering with minimal effort. The most recent of these on the user's end is Mowser.com, developed by Russell Beattie, formerly of Yahoo! Mobile. Basically a user enters a web address and then Mowser dynamically serves up the site with pages that have been reformatted and compressed for mobile. Skweezer.net, a mobile web service pioneered by Greenlight Wireless Corporation, has offered a similar service since 2001.

Over in the developer's chair, Mike Davidson's "two-minute" mobile mod (http://www.mikeindustries.com/blog/archive/2005/07/make-your-site-mobile-friendly) allows site owners to repurpose an existing site with a domain mirror coupled with global_prepend and global_append PHP files.

Figure 3-4. My portfolio page as rendered with Mowser. (Nokia 6680, Symbian OS browser)

While this method may be attractive given its ease of implementation, it does little to address contextual relevance. Further, file size may still be excessive, as markup and text-only content can still be heavyweights in their own right, often resulting in long, scrollable pages with large file sizes. (Keep in mind many mobile subscribers throughout the world pay per KB for data access.) Realistically, it makes little sense to expend development resources on this method, as users are better off using services such as Mowser and Skweezer to do reduce images and styling on their own.

Advantages of this method:

• Relies on the implicit hierarchy in HTML markup

• Readily viewable by a variety of user devices, and (generally) a faster download

• Many mobile browsers override a fair share of styling anyway, begging the question, "Why bother with it?"

Disadvantages of this method:

• Ignores the contextual relevance of mobility

• File size may still be excessive—markup and text-only content can still be heavyweights in their own right

3. USE HANDHELD STYLE SHEETS

Handheld style sheets have typically been regarded as the poster child of a more mobile-friendly web. Because they're inherent in CSS, this method requires the addition of as little as one additional style sheet to a properly coded site, and only one web address is needed. There's certainly no shortage of resources for handheld style sheet development, and those familiar with XHTML and CSS revel in the flexibility and control of these sister style sheets. For example, the website for Mobile 2.0 Conference (Figure 3-5) uses a single handheld style sheet, and implementation was as simple as a few extra lines of markup and CSS.

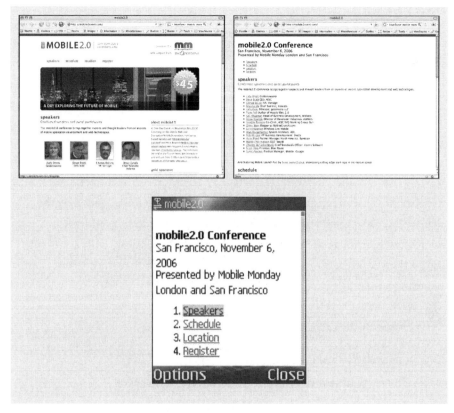

Figure 3-5. *Website for Mobile 2.0 (http://mobile2event.com). Screen CSS version (top left), handheld CSS version previewed in Firefox 2.0 (top right), and handheld CSS version as viewed with Nokia 6680, Symbian OS browser (bottom).*

Referencing a handheld style sheet is as easy as adding the attribute media="handheld" to a style sheet link within the head element:

```
<link href="mobile.css" rel="stylesheet" type="text/css"
    media="handheld" />
```

In a new style sheet, in this example mobile.css, properties are added that reposition or remove unnecessary styling and content from the original markup, such as background images, ads, secondary navigation, as demonstrated with the code that follows.

```
/* Handheld styles */
body {background-image: none;}
#sidebar-ads {display: none;}

...
```

And that's really all there is to it.

However, things aren't as rosy as they seem. `media="handheld"` support on mobile devices is currently hit or miss, more often miss than hit. And even on devices that support it, user data costs may be excessive, as hidden content (i.e. `display:none`) won't display on screen but may still be downloaded by the device. But more importantly, this approach also fails to fully address contextual relevance, as handheld style sheets deal primarily with aesthetics, rather than context, often giving little attention to whether the content is even relevant to mobile browsing.

Advantages of this method:

- Handheld style sheets are inherent in CSS
- Developers maintain as little as one additional style sheet
- Users are presented with a single, unified web address

Disadvantages of this method:

- As with the two previous approaches, this approach ignores the contextual relevance of mobility, as handheld style sheets deal primarily with aesthetics rather than relevance of content
- `media="handheld"` support on mobile devices is currently inconsistent, nearly unreliable

4. CREATE MOBILE-OPTIMIZED CONTENT

As evidenced by the previous methods, an approach that reworks only the aesthetics of web content or ignores mobility typically fails to address the context-, content-, and component-specific needs of mobile users and their devices. This final method addresses first how content is accessed, second what it looks like—context before aesthetics, function before form—by utilizing content adaptation to present users with a customized experience relevant to mobility. Content that isn't feasible for interaction on the go (e.g. website builder) is either removed entirely or adapted to present only mobile-relevant features. New features that leverage mobile device capabilities (e.g. location awareness) are introduced. And overall, pages are usually leaner, sparing excessive data costs and resulting in a faster browsing experience.

Consider the following example. Kayak.com has been quietly climbing the ranks as the Google of travel searches. They don't book flights or hotels, but rather search sites that do, and bring in revenue with paid advertising and search results. Recently Kayak introduced a mobile-optimized version of their site (http://www.kayak.com/moby). Search flights, hotels, even places to eat and you're given quick access to phone numbers and addresses. It doesn't promise more than the context of being mobile offers, and because of that the ensuing experience is satisfying.[2]

Figure 3-6. Kayak Mobile home page using Opera Mini 3.0 on a Nokia 6680.

The Kayak Mobile home page (Figure 3-6) is vastly different from the desktop home page, and it acts only as a category springboard.

Choose "fly" and you're shown a simple screen for entering the departure and arrival airports. Note the simplicity of data input (Figure 3-7). One field facilitates departure and arrival cities using airport codes (or city names), and departure date isn't necessary.

---

[2] A more thorough review of Kayak Mobile, with additional screens and commentary, is available at http://www.cameronmoll.com/archives/001152.html.

When shown the results of your search, you can't book a flight (imagine the data entry on your device!) but you'll get departure and arrival times for flights leaving within the next 24 hours, price, and a phone number to call for reservations . After all, a phone—the device you're most likely using—is primarily an instrument for sending and receiving calls. So naturally, providing the user with a phone number rather than order form is a beautifully simple, contextually relevant solution.

Figure 3-7. Kayak Mobile flight search screen (left) and search results (right).

As contextually relevant as this method purports to be, it also has its issues. The most glaring of these is the much-debated **"One Web"** notion.[3] As defined by those involved in the W3C's Mobile Web Initiative (see http://www.w3.org/Mobile),

> *"... One Web means making, as far as is reasonable, the same information and services available to users **irrespective of the device they are using.** However, it does not mean that exactly the same information is available in exactly the same representation across all devices. The context of mobile use, device capability*

---

[3] Jo Rabin's appropriately titled article, "One Web - Why does this stir up such emotion?" (http://dev.mobi/node/87) explains this conundrum in detail.

variations, bandwidth issues and mobile network capabilities all affect the representation."[4]

"Device," in this context, refers to not only mobile phones, but also desktop machines, screen readers, even cars and watches—any web-enabled device. Mobile-optimized content is often audience- and device-centric. The underlying argument by proponents of One Web is to be cautious about denying access to content by making assumptions about the user and his or her device. For example, if you've selectively hidden portions of your content by assuming mobile users prefer content that differs from the desktop, what happens when the user owns a mobile device that is fully capable of rendering content the same as a desktop machine?

Other drawbacks may include developers maintaining two sets of files (desktop, mobile) and users being required to bookmark and recall alternate web addresses for the same content (i.e. one for desktop, one for mobile).

Advantages of this method:

- Contextually relevant—addresses first how content is consumed, second what it looks like
- Pages are usually leaner, so users are spared excessive bandwidth costs and generally enjoy a faster browsing experience

Disadvantages of this method:

- Denies access to content by making assumptions about the user and his or her device
- Developers may need to maintain two sets of files (desktop, mobile)
- Alternate web addresses are often required, which places a burden on users to bookmark and recall more than one web address for the same content

---

4 W3C, "Mobile Web Best Practices 1.0," http://www.w3.org/TR/mobile-bp/#OneWeb.

WHICH METHOD IS BEST?

So, which of these methods is best for your particular project? If only there were a clear winner among the four methods presented here! Alas, the "It Depends" maxim rears its ugly head, and your strategy will likely depend on such criteria as user goals and objectives, development resources, and the content depth and breadth of your website or application.

If I were to remove my Unbiased Author hat for a moment, but only a brief moment, to offer my opinion of the four methods I've outlined, I might say that reducing images and styling seems an unnecessary development endeavor. And I might say it's debatable whether handheld CSS will ever be of any value to developers and users, despite its promising aspirations. On the other hand, I just might say **doing nothing and mobile-optimized content are emerging as the two most viable approaches.** I see the two co-existing for the next couple years as new devices and browsers enter the market offering great content zooming experiences but also leveraging mobile-exclusive technology such as location awareness and camera/video capabilities.

Hat reaffixed.

XHTML/CSS DEVELOPMENT

IN THE EARLY YEARS OF MOBILE web publishing and up until fairly recently, Wireless Markup Language (WML), an XML-based content language developed in 1999, was the de facto standard for publishing mobile web content. Despite requiring web developers to learn a new language based on a deck and card metaphor[1], it did in fact provide a much-needed global standard for developers by consolidating some of the disparate, proprietary markup languages in use at the time by Ericsson, Nokia, and Openwave.[2]

WML, however, is no longer considered the global standard for mobile web development. Its decline in recent years has given way to XHTML-based content, which yields a much smaller learning curve for designers and developers and effectively bridges the gap between desktop and mobile environments.

WAP 2.0: AN XHTML ENVIRONMENT

Let's begin with a few basic tenets of mobile internet technology: **Wireless Application Protocol (WAP)** is the protocol for enabling mobile access to internet content. **Wireless Markup Language (WML)** is the language for

---

[1] For a primer on WML, see W3School's "Introduction to WAP," http://www.w3schools.com/wap/wap_intro.asp.

[2] Luca Passani, "History of XHTML Mobile Profile," http://developer.openwave.com/dvl/support/documentation/guides_and_references/xhtml-mp_style_guide/chapter1.htm.

ith WAP 2.0, **XHTML Mobile Profile (XHTML-MP)** is the preferred markup language, and **XHTML Basic** is an acceptable alternative.

Nearly all devices sold anywhere in the world today support WAP 2.0, and while the specification for WAP 2.0 strongly recommends that supporting devices offer backwards compatibility for WML, it doesn't require that developers provide a WML edition of their content in addition to their XHTML edition. Some devices, such as the Apple iPhone, support nearly any form of HTML over the standard HTTP protocol or WAP.

In short, **WAP 1.0 = WML, WAP 2.0 = XHTML.**

At this point you should be slapping yourself upside the head, exclaiming "Ah ha!" as you realize you have all the basic coding knowledge you need to begin developing mobilized websites and applications. In the words of authors at DevelopersHome.com, "With the announcement of XHTML Mobile Profile, the markup language of the wireless world and the wired world finally converges.... The greatest advantage, however, is that the same technologies can now be used to develop both the web and wireless version of your Internet site."

This concept of convergence is what makes WAP 2.0 appealing to traditional desktop web developers. Whether you choose to develop with XHTML Basic or XHTML-MP, both are merely subsets of XHTML and therefore not a far cry from XHTML Transitional or Strict.[3] And because each is a subset of XHTML, initial testing and validation can be done within most desktop browsers. Thorough, final testing will certainly need to be conducted using actual devices, but at the very least you can test initially within a desktop browser to see if the markup renders correctly and semantically—a luxury not afforded by WML.

---

[3] There has been considerable debate about whether XHTML Basic or XHTML-MP should be the recognized language for WAP 2.0, but for all intents and purposes the two languages are almost identical and are rendered equally well by most devices. A comparison chart of XHTML Basic and XHTML MP can be found at http://dev.mobi/node/119.

However, a word of caution: **For some devices, don't expect markup to render or even behave the same way you're used to in the desktop environment.** First, there are literally dozens of mobile browsers on the market, each rendering markup in often widely varying formats. (Trust me, battling with a half-dozen desktop browsers won't seem so bad after wrestling with a couple dozen mobile browsers.) Second, not all HTML elements and CSS properties are supported, nor should they be in some situations. For example, the CSS float property isn't supported by a number of mobile browsers, and at the same time it's somewhat impractical to use floats when dealing with a screen that may be only 128 pixels wide.[4]

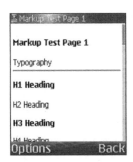 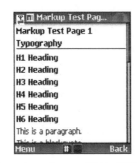 

Figure 4-1. *How heading elements render on a Nokia 6680 (Symbian OS browser left, Opera Mini right) and on a Treo 650 (Blazer 4.0 browser).*

In 2005, I set out to reveal the markup rendering differences from browser to browser by creating a series of **Markup Test Pages** (http://www.cameronmoll.com/mobile/mkp) aimed at demonstrating how HTML elements and CSS properties would perform. I enlisted participation from about 15 individuals with various devices, and analysis following device testing by these individuals led to the recommendations in **Mobile Web Design: Tips & Techniques** (http://www.cameronmoll.com/archives/000577.html). Figure 4-1 contains a few results from Markup Test Page 1 (typography). Shown are

---

[4] While floats may be impractical, it's interesting to note that my Nokia 6800, a device I purchased back in 2004 and whose screen is a mere 128 pixels wide, supports floats rather well.

just three browsers on just two devices, and yet note the visual disparity of heading size and bolding.

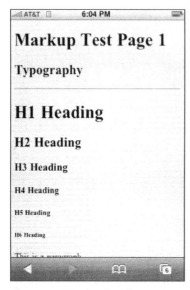

Figure 4-2. How heading elements render on an iPhone with the native browser.

Alternately, because iPhone includes a minimized version of the Safari browser, dubbed "MobileSafari," it supports heading size and bolding as you'd expect (Figure 4-2).

In summary, because many devices in the market today support standards-based markup, feel free to be liberal with your HTML and CSS usage within the mobile environment. But be sure to include thorough testing during and upon completion of development (see chapter that follows, **Testing & Validation**).

MOBILE WEB STANDARDS

Ask 10 web developers what "web standards" means and you'll get 10 different answers. Thus, I defer to The Devil's Dictionary to act as definitive voice:

> **"web standards,** noun - A large stick or cudgel, used by the slightly more anal-retentive to beat the slightly less anal-retentive."

On a more serious note, Roger Johansson offers the following definition:

> "Web standards are technologies, established by the W3C and other standards bodies, that are used to create and interpret web-based content. These technologies are designed to future-proof documents

published on the Web and to make those documents accessible to as many as possible."

The important point here is that these technologies (standards) apply to *all* web content, including mobile. **Consequently, there's really no need to establish new standards just for the mobile web.** The underlying standards for the greater web, regardless of device, person, or place, are the same: semantic markup, separation of structure and presentation, accessibility, and so on.

What is needed, however, are recommendations and best practices for mobile. The W3C's Mobile Web Initiative (MWI) is doing much to promote recommendations for delivering content to mobile devices through its Best Practices Working Group. The most notable document published by this group thus far is **Mobile Web Best Practices 1.0,** available at http:// www.w3.org/TR/mobile-bp. Compiled with input from mobile developers and industry-leading organizations, the document "specifies Best Practices for delivering Web content to mobile devices" with the principle objective to "improve the user experience of the Web when accessed from mobile devices."

An alternative to these recommendations—or a complement, depending on how you look at it—is **Global Authoring Practices for the Mobile Web** (http://www.passani.it/gap), authored by mobile expert Luca Passani. As one of the early contributors to the Best Practices Working Group, Luca became dissatisfied with recommendations made by the group and eventually published his own set of recommendations based on years of experience in mobile development.

Whether you agree or disagree with the advice offered by the Best Practices Working Group and Luca Passani, both parties offer recommendations worth considering.

FUNDAMENTAL MARKUP STRUCTURE

*Note: The following recommendations are applicable if you've chosen method #4, Mobile-Optimized Content (see previous chapter, **Four Methods, Revisited**). These recommendations assume you've chosen XHTML-MP over XHTML Basic, although the markup structure is very similar for both subset languages.*

That precious moment has arrived, wherein one's heart palpitates at the thought of opening one's favorite text editor and flawlessly composing line upon line of clean, semantic markup. Or wherein one's palms sweat upon realizing one must churn out line after line of complex elements, attributes, properties, and values.

Either way, it's time to put some markup beneath your content. Shown here is the recommended basic markup structure for a well-formatted XHTML-MP document, followed by a description of the individual components. (Note: Left arrow (↵) indicates line wrapping.)

```
 1. <?xml version="1.0" encoding="UTF-8" ?>
 2. <!DOCTYPE html PUBLIC "-//WAPFORUM//DTD XHTML Mobile ↵
    1.0//EN"
 3.   "http://www.wapforum.org/DTD/xhtml-mobile10.dtd">
 4.
 5. <html xmlns="http://www.w3.org/1999/xhtml">
 6. <head>
 7.   <title>My Site's Title</title>
 8.   <link rel="stylesheet" type="text/css" ↵
    href="mobile.css"/>
 9.   <meta http-equiv="Cache-Control" content="max-age=600" />
10. </head>
11.
12. <body>
13.   <h1>My Page Heading</h1>
```

```
14.    <p>My content goes here.</p>
15.  </body>
16.  </html>
```

Line 1 is the **character encoding** for the document.[5] The recommendation here is to use UTF-8 encoding for maximum compatibility (see http://dev.mobi/node/341).

Lines 2 and 3 are the **DOCTYPE**, short for "document type declaration," which tells a validator which version of (X)HTML to use when checking the document's syntax. Shown here is the recommended DOCTYPE for XHTML-MP.

Line 5 is the recommended XHTML **namespace**.

Line 8 is the directive for linking to your mobile-specific **style sheet**. See section that follows for additional CSS information.

Line 9 is the **cache control header**, which instructs the browser to use a local copy instead of requesting a new copy from the server if the local copy has not expired (see http://dev.mobi/node/209). In this example, the expiry time is 10 minutes (600 seconds), but you should adjust this value according to how often your content is updated. Cache control can be helpful for reducing page refreshing on slower mobile networks.

Once you've made it to the body, the XHTML-MP markup is not unlike what you're already used to with XHTML Transitional or Strict. As you begin development, keep a browser tab open with DevelopersHome.com's **XHTML-MP Tutorial** (http://www.developershome.com/wap/xhtmlmp), an impressively replete resource for all things XHTML-MP.

---

[5] If this were a page created for desktop browsers, you would not include this XML declaration, as pages that have an XML declaration before the DOCTYPE force IE 6 to use quirks mode.

Figure 4-3. English 360 Mobile as viewed with a Sony Ericsson K750i using the native NetFront browser.

You'll probably need a complete list of XHTML-MP elements and accompanying attributes whilst furiously coding your critical content, so keep another tab open with the **XHTML-MP Tags List** found at http://htmllint.itc.keio.ac.jp/htmllint/tagslist.cgi?HTMLVersion=XHTML-MP.

Should you need a little inspiration along the way, browse to and view the source of the following mobilized sites. Not all of these follow the markup structure precisely as shown here but utilize relatively good markup nonetheless.

- **Flickr Mobile:** http://flickr.com/mob
- **Fandango Mobile:** http://mobile.fandango.com
- **Popurls Mobile:** http://popurls.mobi
- **English360 Mobile** (Figure 4-3), archived copy: http://cameronmoll.com/mobile/e360

Once you've got the basics down, dive deeper into best practices, coding tips, and mobile usability recommendations with these resources:

- **Mobile Style Guides - Screen Design, Part 1** by Barbara Ballard: http://www.littlespringsdesign.com/design/styleguides/sampleguide/sampleguide3
- **Global Authoring Practices for the Mobile Web** by Luca Passani: http://www.passani.it/gap
- **dotMobi Mobile Web Developer's Guide:** http://dev.mobi/node/293

Finally, if you're lucky enough to develop for iPhone users only, begin with Apple's **Optimizing Web Applications and Content for iPhone** (http://

developer.apple.com/iphone/designingcontent.html) followed by **iPhoneWebDev** (http://iphonewebdev.com). Other notable resources include John Gruber's **iPhone Fonts From Mac OS X** (http://daringfireball.net/misc/2007/07/iphone-osx-fonts) and Joe Hewitt's **iUI** (http://www.joehewitt.com/iui), a JavaScript and CSS bundle aimed at making iPhone web app development easier:

> *"As much as possible, iUI maps common HTML idioms to iPhone interface conventions. For example, the <ul> and <li> tags are used to create hierarchical side-scrolling navigation. Ordinary <a> links load with a sliding animation while keeping you on the original page instead of loading an entirely new one. A simple set of CSS classes can be used to designate things like modal dialogs, preference panels, and on/off switches."*

Off you go, heart palpitating or sweaty palms in tow.

MOBILE CSS

Admittedly, the current state of CSS support by many mobile browsers leaves much to be desired. Only about half of the CSS properties you're comfortable using will be transferrable to mobile. The other half are supported either too poorly to use or not at all.

While in need of an update, many of the CSS observations in "Mobile Web Design: Tips & Techniques" are still applicable today, some of which include the following:

- font-size will be ignored by most browsers; consider using headings (h1, h2, h3) instead to control font sizing
- font-family will also be ignored by most browsers, as nearly all devices currently default to their own proprietary sans-serif

- `background-image` support is marginal, while `background-color` is somewhat well supported
- `border-style` support overall is sketchy, but `border-style: solid` is probably the most reliable value
- `margin` and `padding` support is decent, though very poor on some devices; use cautiously with small screen real estate

As for including or linking to CSS in your pages, your options are the same as for desktop sites: external, embedded, and inline. Some experts argue embedded or inline over external in favor of reducing the number of HTTP connections per page request, yet experience shows many popular mobilized sites and apps employ external linking without issue. (Note: When using external linking, `<link>` is the most widely supported as compared to the `<?xml-stylesheet?>` and `@import` directives.)

It should be noted that there also exists CSS Mobile Profile 2.0, for which the working draft "defines in general a subset of CSS 2.1 that is to be considered a baseline for interoperability between implementations of CSS on constrained devices (e.g. mobile phones)." Surprisingly, the draft document is legible and fairly easy to read (Figure 4-4), in contrast to other draft documents penned by the W3C. Child selectors and even some pseudo-classes are proposed to be supported by mobile browsers, but therein lies the problem. Browser developers must adhere to and support the recommended specifications, build them into their browsers, and users in turn must own devices with these CSS 2.1-compliant browsers installed—a cycle that will inevitably take some time before yielding a market majority.

For a comparison of the various flavors of mobile CSS, see http://dev.mobi/node/154.

In the meantime, the recommendation provided earlier still stands: Feel free to be liberal with your HTML and CSS usage within the mobile environment, but be sure to include thorough testing during and upon completion of development.

Selector type	Example	Meaning
Universal selector	*	Matches any element.
Type selectors	E	Matches any E element.
Descendant selectors	E F	Matches any F element that is a descendant of an E element.
Child selectors	E > F	Matches any F element that is a child of an element E.
The link pseudo-classes	E:link	Matches element E if E is the source anchor of a hyperlink, unvisited by a user.
The link pseudo-classes	E:visited	Matches element E if E is the source anchor of a hyperlink, visited by a user.
The dynamic pseudo-classes	E:active	Matches element E if E is being activated by the user.
The dynamic pseudo-classes	E:focus	Matches element E if E has the focus (accepts keyboard events or other forms of text input).
Class selectors	.warning	*Language specific.* (In (X)HTML, matches elements whose class attribute contains a token with the same name.)
ID selectors	#myid	Matches any element with an ID equal to "myid".
Grouping	E1, E2, E3 { ... }	Matches a group of elements, which share the same style declarations.

Figure 4-4. Selectors table for CSS Mobile Profile showing which selector constructs must be supported by mobile browsers among those defined by CSS 2.1.

DEVICE DETECTION

During the process of creating mobile-optimized content, you'll inevitably confront the need to deliver this content to users without requiring them to remember or type a complex mobile web address. One solution is to create a new mobile-specific web address, such as a yahoo.mobi (see final chapter, **Promoting Your Content**). Another solution is to detect the type of device requesting the content, and if it's a mobile device, the user is redirected to mobile content.

The latter solution is commonly referred to as device detection, and it requires no effort on the users' part—they simply enter the same address they're familiar with, such as yahoo.com, and a mobile version is automatically shown. Every user agent (browser)—whether mobile, desktop, or other—is characterized by a unique user agent string, accept values, and headers. Device detection essentially "sniffs" these characteristics, and if they are determined to ₐₚₗₑₛₑₙₜ a mobile device, the browser is instructed to redirect to an alternate web address or sub-directory, which typically houses a mobile-friendly version of the content.

One of the most common methods of device detection involves the use of the Wireless Universal Resource File (http://wurfl.sourceforge.net), also known as WURFL.[6] Developed by Luca Passani and Andrea Trasatti, WURFL is a robust XML file that contains information regarding the configurations, capabilities, and features of nearly every device on the planet.

A less complex method, but nearly as reliable as WURFL for detecting mobile devices, involves a simple PHP script written by Andy Moore, dotMobi Certified Mobile Web Developer. With his permission, included on the following pages is his script with explanatory comments. This script is offered under a shared source license and may be downloaded at http://www.andymoore.info/download-manager.php?id=13. (Note: Left arrow (↵) indicates line wrapping.)

The first portion of this script creates the function name detect_mobile_device() and then performs the first of five checks:

```
1.  <?php
2.
3.  function detect_mobile_device(){
4.  // check 1: check if the user agent value claims to be
5.  // windows but not windows mobile
6.  if(stristr($_SERVER['HTTP_USER_AGENT'],'windows')&&!↵
        stristr($_SERVER['HTTP_USER_AGENT'],'windows ce')){
7.      return false;
8.  }
```

---

[6] For an introductory tutorial on WURFL, see "Introduction to WURFL" (http://dev.mobi/node/18) by Andrea Trasatti.

The sum of these five checks attempts to detect the unique user agent string, accept values, and headers to determine if the requesting agent is a mobile browser.[7] The first two checks detect the user agent string, the former detects the difference between Windows and Windows Mobile, and the latter detects any obvious signs of a mobile browser:

```
 9. // check 2: check if the user agent gives away any
10. // tell tale signs it's a mobile browser
11. if(eregi('up.browser|up.link|windows ce|iemobile|↵
    mini|mmp|symbian|midp|wap|phone|pocket|mobile|pda|psp',↵
    $_SERVER['HTTP_USER_AGENT'])){
12.    return true;
13. }
```

The third check detects the http_accept header:

```
14. // check 3: check the http accept header to see if
15. // wap.wml or wap.xhtml support is claimed
16. if(stristr($_SERVER['HTTP_ACCEPT'],'text/vnd.wap.wml')||↵
    stristr($_SERVER['HTTP_ACCEPT'],↵
    'application/vnd.wap.xhtml+xml')){
17.    return true;
18. }
```

The fourth check detects the _server header:

```
19. // check 4: check if there are any tell tales signs
20. // it's a mobile device from the _server headers
```

---

[7] If you're interested in seeing these characteristics displayed, visit the following page, developed by dotMobi Director of Standards Jo Rabin, with your mobile device or desktop browser: http://rabin.mobi/http.

```
21. if(isset($_SERVER['HTTP_X_WAP_PROFILE'])||↵
    isset($_SERVER['HTTP_PROFILE'])||↵
    isset($_SERVER['X-OperaMini-Features'])||↵
    isset($_SERVER['UA-pixels'])){
22.   return true;
23. }
```

The fifth and final check detects the user agent and matches it against a list of known mobile browsers:

```
24. // build an array with the first four characters from
25. // the most common mobile user agents
26. $a = ↵
    array('acs-','alav','alca','amoi','audi','aste','avan',↵
    'benq','bird','blac','blaz','brew','cell','cldc','cmd-',↵
    'dang','doco','eric','hipt','inno','ipaq','java','jigs',↵
    'kddi','keji','leno','lg-c','lg-d','lg-g','lge-','maui',↵
    'maxo','midp','mits','mmef','mobi','mot-','moto','mwbp',↵
    'nec-','newt','noki','opwv','palm','pana','pant','pdxg',↵
    'phil','play','pluc','port','prox','qtek','qwap','sage',↵
    'sams','sany','sch-','sec-','send','seri','sgh-','shar',↵
    'sie-','siem','smal','smar','sony','sph-','symb','t-mo',↵
    'teli','tim-','tosh','tsm-','upg1','upsi','vk-v','voda',↵
    'w3c','wap-','wapa','wapi','wapp','wapr','webc','winw',↵
    'winw','xda','xda-');
27. // check 5: check if the first four characters of the
28. // current user agent are set as a key in the array
29. if(isset($a[substr($_SERVER['HTTP_USER_AGENT'],0,4)])){
30.   return true;
31. }
32. }
```

For the checks that return a value of true, the script assumes it has correctly identified a mobile browser. If false is returned, the script is also used to detect and redirect desktop browsers. Both examples are included in the closing lines of the script:

```
33. // example 1 - detect and redirect mobile browsers
34. if(detect_mobile_device()){
35.    header('Location: http://yoursite.mobi/');
36.    exit;
37. }
38.
39. // example 2 - detect and redirect desktop browsers
40. if(!detect_mobile_device()){
41.    header('Location: http://yoursite.com/');
42.    exit();
43. }
```

And that's it. Users are now redirected and land safely on a new page, awash with mobile goodness.

However, it's worth noting device detection doesn't come without drawbacks. Device detection is rarely 100% reliable, even though in many cases it may be good enough. User agents are occasionally incorrectly reported, and any resource files such as WURFL must be updated as new devices with new user agents enter the market. Device detection often results in device fragmentation, i.e. content formatted specifically for an individual device or range of devices, and therefore developers must maintain multiple sets of files as devices are introduced, updated, or eliminated. Further, and more importantly, you're choosing on the user's behalf what he or she can or cannot see. What if the user's device is capable of rendering a rich internet experience, and yet you've selectively "dumbed down" the content?

Consider these issues and others before deciding to proceed with device detection.

TESTING & VALIDATION

IF THERE'S ONE QUESTION THAT TENDS to be repeated more than any other, it's undoubtedly about testing for mobile devices. Many designers and developers new to mobile development are perplexed by the procedures used for testing web content on mobile devices and often don't even know where to begin. Fortunately, it's a lot easier than most expect, and following are methods for testing and validating with and without handsets in hand.

TESTING WITH SOFTWARE

When using XHTML for mobile web documents, you have a number of options at your disposal to conduct initial testing and validation before ever picking up a mobile device. These options are threefold: Desktop browsers, web-based emulators, and desktop emulators.

Although any desktop browser will offer a rendered preview of your content, two browsers offer tools specific to mobile development (Figure 5-1). Using the **Web Developer Toolbar** (https://addons.mozilla.org/firefox/addon/60) compatible with the Firefox browser, open your file and select Miscellaneous > Small Screen Rendering. The window width will be reduced to roughly 260 px and the layout will be reformatted to simulate rendering by a mobile browser.

The same can be accomplished using the Opera browser by selecting View > Small screen.[1]

The **User Agent Switcher extension** for Firefox (https://addons.mozilla.org/firefox/addon/59) is also helpful for emulating the user agent string for mobile browsers. You need to manually add new strings, and you can do so with this list of popular mobile user agent strings: http://www.zytrax.com/tech/web/mobile_ids.html. Combined with the Web Developer Toolbar's Small Screen Rendering, User Agent Switcher can provide a decent glimpse of how your content will be rendered for as many strings (phones) as you choose.

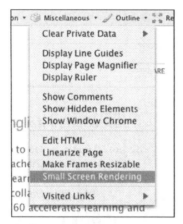 

Figure 5-1. Simulating a small screen using the Firefox Web Developer Toolbar (left) and Opera 9 (right).

Next in line are web-based emulators, which enable you to view content rendering with greater accuracy than desktop browsers. The **dotMobi Emulator** (http://emulator.mtld.mobi) currently offers simulation for the Sony Ericsson K750 and Nokia N70 devices. The **Opera Mini Simulator** (http://www.operamini.com/demo) provides a preview of the Opera Mini browser, which is compatible with dozens of devices. Kyle Barrow's **Mimic** (http://pukupi.com/tools/mimic) emulates the N400i (European) or N505i (Japanese)

---

[1] If you use handheld CSS, for both of these methods window width will not be resized but instead the handheld version of your file will be displayed.

i-mode mobiles. And **DeviceAnywhere** (http://deviceanywhere.com) offers the most robust emulation, with access to more than 300 devices for a monthly fee starting at US $200.

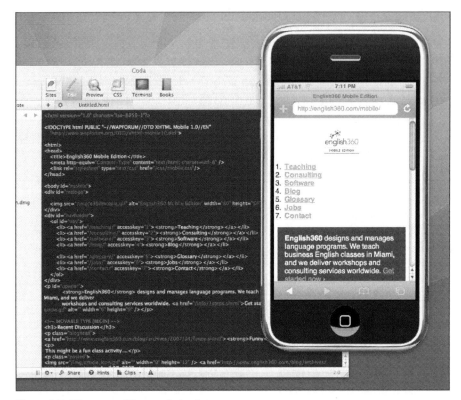

Figure 5-2. iPhoney, an iPhone web simulator.

Lastly, desktop software is available should desktop browsers and web-based emulators not suffice. Nokia (Symbian) and Openwave, two of the most widely used mobile browsers, offer software development kits for their respective browsers:

- **Nokia Mobile Browser Simulator:** http://mobilewebbook.com/shorty/66307

- **Openwave Phone Simulator:** http://mobilewebbook.com/shorty/93271

Another option is **SmartPhone Emulator Developer Edition** (http://www.yospace.com/spede.html) by Yospace Technologies Ltd., compatible with Windows, Linux, and Mac. SmartPhone Emulator provides XHTML-MP and i-mode simulation for more than 45 handsets.

Chances are you'll need to test for iPhone as well. **iPhoney** (http://www.marketcircle.com/iphoney) is a free iPhone web simulator (Figure 5-2) currently compatible only with Mac OS X.

TESTING WITH DEVICES

As useful as emulators are, they regrettably provide only approximate emulation and not wholly accurate rendering. For that, you must rely on actual mobile devices. With several hundred devices in the market today, testing your content on every available model is not only impractical but also nearly impossible.

However, it's possible to do relatively accurate testing with as little as 5-10 devices, if evidenced by efforts from one of the largest sites on the web. During the summer of 2006, Yahoo! partnered with FIFA to provide a mobile-friendly experience for the official FIFA World Cup website (http://fifaworldcup.com). Yahoo!, who reports that more than 379 million of its users are also mobile device owners[2], understood the daunting task of providing content to millions of users with hundreds of handset models, yet they weren't overwhelmed by the challenge. In fact, their approach for testing was incredibly simple, as described by Joe

Figure 5-3. *The official FIFA World Cup 2006 website. (Nokia 6680, Symbian OS browser)*

---

[2] Barry Schwartz, "Mobile Search," http://www.seroundtable.com/archives/002330.html

Shepter in his case study, **Yahoo! FIFA Mobile Site** (http://
www.designinteract.com/features/yahoofifa):

> *"To make sense of the chaos, Yahoo!'s team first selected a target
> group of ten phones. They were all widely distributed, and their
> browsers ran the gamut from high-end to barely functional. As the
> thinking went, if the site worked perfectly on all of them, it would
> perform reasonably well on the rest of the world's phones."*

With just 10 widely varying devices, Yahoo! successfully tested its content for a
global audience, and the resulting site (Figure 5-3) drew an astounding 5.3
million unique visitors and nearly 290 million page views at its highest daily
peak.[3]

Getting your hands on 5-10 widely varying devices isn't insurmountable. First,
consider using devices already within reach. You shouldn't have a difficult time
getting at least 3-5 disparate phones on temporary loan from friends and
colleagues for an hour or two at a time. Second, if you've got a blog, don't
hesitate to ask for volunteers. I did and the results were great. Finally, consider
purchasing several devices to have on hand. If you or a team member has a
data plan with a carrier or operator that uses SIM cards[4], for around US
$1,000 you can equip your team with 3-5 devices by purchasing unlocked
phones on eBay (do a search for "unlocked phone") and then swap the SIM
card among the devices when testing.

Equally important, if not more important, as testing with actual devices is
testing with actual users. Not only is visual rendering of your content essential
but user interaction with it, as well—a critical analysis that can't always be

---

[3] comScore Press Release, "'Group of Death' Finale Drives Record Visitation and Page Views
to Official FIFA World Cup Web Site on Thursday, June 22," June 28, 2006, http://
www.comscore.com/press/release.asp?press=922.

[4] In the U.S., major carriers that use SIM cards include AT&T and T-Mobile. In Europe,
major operators that use SIM cards include O2, Orange, T-Mobile, Vodaphone, and others.

accomplished with emulators and in-house testing alone. Most user testing will be conducted indoors in a controlled environment, but it's also wise to consider contextual factors such as direct sunlight and the resulting screen contrast or lack thereof, one-handed data entry, page flow with network latency while moving, and so on.

When testing indoors, there are a number of methods for conducting, displaying, and recording user testing. **Project-a-Phone** (http://www.projectaphone.com) is an imaging device that can dock nearly any device and then relay video to a PC via USB cable. For Symbian Series 60 and Series 80 devices, **ImageExpo** (http://www.sysopendigia.com/C2256FEF0043E9C1/0/405001172) relays video to a PC or projector via Bluetooth. For BlackBerry devices, **Blackberry Viewer** (http://www.idokorro.com/products/bbviewer.shtml) does the same via USB cable.

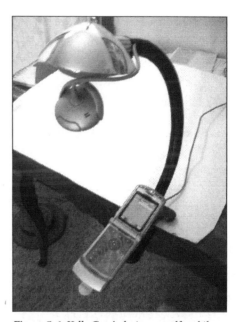

Figure 5-4. Kelly Goto's do-it-yourself mobile testing cam. (Image copyright Kelly Goto. Used by permission.)

If you're a do-it-yourselfer, Kelly Goto's **DIY Mobile Cam** (http://www.gotomobile.com/archives/diy-gotomobiles-mobile-cam) offers complete instructions for building your own imaging device using a gooseneck lamp and ordinary web cam (Figure 5-4). If you own a Mac, you can create a similar setup by purchasing a used **iSight** camera and **SightFlex** (gooseneck stand for iSight) on eBay, and then a copy of **iGlasses** (http://www.ecamm.com/mac/iglasses) to enhance and rotate or mirror the output image.

VALIDATION

Validation, simply stated, checks conformance with W3C recommendations and other standards to ensure your content can be properly rendered by browsers. While it's considered good practice to produce valid markup regardless, it becomes critical when mobile browsers are added to the mix. On average, mobile browsers aren't nearly as forgiving with poorly formatted markup as are desktop browsers. In fact, your content might look fine when viewed using some of the desktop browser methods mentioned earlier in this chapter, only to fail to render at all when viewed with a mobile browser (Figure 5-5). When this occurs, more often than not it's because your code doesn't validate.

Figure 5-5. Popurls Mobile (http:// popurls.mobi), which aggregates headlines from other popular news and aggregate sites, occasionally fails to render due to markup errors in the content they embed. (Treo 650, Blazer 4.0 browser)

"The good news," as stated by mobile analyst Dennis Bourique in his article **Validation is Your Friend** (http:// wapreview.com/blog/?p=184), "is that if your markup is valid and page size is under 20 KB (including images) your site will load and display without errors on 99% of WAP2 browsers." Dennis cites the most common errors as being unencoded ampersands in text and URLs, improper tag nesting, and unclosed tags—similar errors common to desktop web development. These errors and others can be snuffed out with a simple pass through the W3C Validator, the same one you've already been using with other web documents.[5]

Two additional resources that are helpful aren't validators per se but rather services that offer compatibility reports measured against recommendations from sponsoring organizations. The **Mobile Web Best Practices Checker** (http://validator.w3.org/mobile) scrutinizes markup to see how well it conforms to guidelines in the W3C's Mobile Web Best Practices. dotMobi's **ready.mobi** is an all-in-one service of sorts, offering conformance analysis, emulation previews, estimated data costs and speeds for users, and more (Figure 5-6).

---

[5] Because the W3C recommends XHTML Basic be used instead of XHTML-MP, their validator tends to be picky with XHTML-MP documents, especially when served with the MIME type `text/html`. More about XHTML-MP and proper MIME types can be found here: http://www.developershome.com/wap/xhtmlmp/xhtml_mp_tutorial.asp? page=mimeTypesFileExtension.

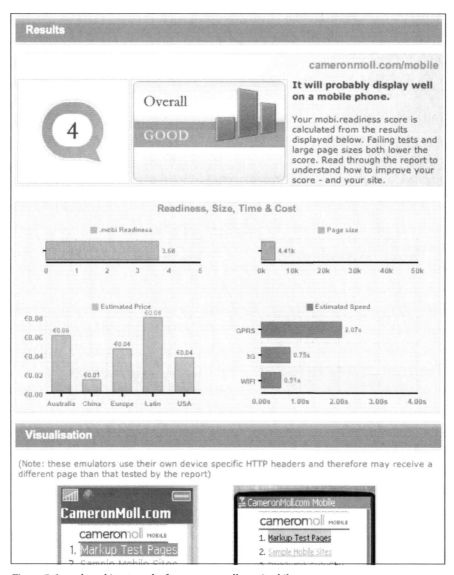

Figure 5-6. ready.mobi test results for cameronmoll.com/mobile.

BEYOND SIMPLE XHTML PAGES

WHEN DEVELOPING CONTENT FOR MOBILE DEVICES, it's important to look beyond simple XHTML/CSS pages and even beyond the browser. The interplay between web content and mobile user can occur in a variety of ways, some of which are often more efficient, affordable, or universal than browser-based interaction—even some of which are not delivered through the web but through other content delivery channels. This chapter exposes a few approaches for developing a well-rounded mobile strategy.

MESSAGING

Mobile messaging, quite simply, is a far more prevalent mobile activity than viewing web content with a browser. To ignore messaging is to ignore the largest slice of the content consumer pie and a potentially profitable opportunity. Messaging comes in a variety of flavors: **Short Messaging Service (SMS),** which is text-only messaging; **Multimedia Messaging Service (MMS)** for sending photos, audio, video, and rich text in addition to plain text; **Enhanced Messaging Service (EMS),** a technology older and less capable than MMS, but marginally more capable than SMS.

Of particular interest as it relates to mobile web content is text messaging. More than 10 billion text messages are sent worldwide every month, and estimates for SMS support on handsets in use today range as high as 98%.[1] In the U.K. alone, 41.8 billion text messages were sent in 2006.[2] Because of its prevalence, person-to-person (one-to-one) text messaging is a familiar activity: A user types a message on her handset, sends it to a personal number, and the intended recipient receives the message on his handset. However, texting can also be a one-to-many or many-to-one relationship. Content providers big and small have leveraged the power of texting as a means of serving web content to mobile users in this way. For example, mobile users can conduct a web search by texting their search query rather than entering a query in a browser search field.

Figure 6-1. Using Google SMS Search with a Nokia 6800 in my trusty Jeep Cherokee. (Yes, of course I was parked.)

---

[1] CellSigns, "Text Messaging Statistics," http://www.cellsigns.com/industry.shtml.

[2] Text.it, "41.8 Billion Text Messages For 2006," http://www.text.it/mediacentre/press_release_list.cfm?thePublicationID=351A37F2-C5A0-881E-03C5B18AAC2AE745.

Google SMS offers SMS search, and the process combines texting and search query (Figure 6-1). A user types keywords, e.g. "hotels san francisco," as a text message, sends the message to Google's SMS number (466453 in the U.S.), and search results are sent back as a text message. Only a few relevant results are sent, often as multiple text messages due to the recommended 160 character limit for SMS messages. **Yahoo! oneSearch** and **4INFO.net** offer similar services, among others.

PayPal has also embraced texting as a means for extending its popular web payment service to mobile phones. PayPal's **Text To Buy** allows consumers to send money via phone merely by texting an amount and email address to PayPal's SMS number, which is 729725 in the U.S. (Figure 6-2). In addition to texting, **PayPal Mobile Checkout** offers PayPal's traditional payment services via mobile browser.

PayPal's Text To Buy. (Nokia 6680)

SMS search and Text To Buy are only the tip of the proverbial texting iceberg. Imagine if the University of Texas directory (see chapter, **Mobile Web Fundamentals**) were also available by SMS. One could text "amy miller" to a number for the university and receive matching directory results by text message. The options are seemingly endless for employing text messaging to serve web content. Although I personally recommend you seek professional assistance if considering a custom messaging solution, DevelopersHome.com offers a very thorough **SMS Tutorial** at http://www.developershome.com/sms. A less replete but more digestible overview is **How SMS Works** by Howstuffworks.com, located at http://communication.howstuffworks.com/sms.htm.

The SMS numbers mentioned thus far—Google (466453), PayPal (729725)—are commonly known as **Short Codes.** They differ from phone numbers in that they act as a numeric domain name for text messaging, and they're often shorter in length than phone numbers, typically 4-6 digits. The numbers often map to letters (e.g. 82267 = "tacos"), much like toll-free advertising phone numbers.

However, while Short Codes function irrespective of carrier or operator, they are not as universal as domain names because they are generally restricted to continents. So while 466453 is the Short Code for Google in the U.S., in the U.K. the Short Code may be an entirely different number. Further, because Short Codes are meant to be short, the quantity of available codes is limited. In North America, for example, Short Codes are five-digit numbers in the range 20000-99999, which results in 79,999 total numbers available.

To register a Short Code, visit one of the following:

- **U.S.:** http://www.usshortcodes.com
- **U.K.:** http://www.short-codes.com

Alternatively, if you are an organization based in the U.S., **TextMarks** (http://www.textmarks.com) offer a generic Short Code (41411) that can be used by any organization to send on-demand, customized messages to users, such as a web address, a marketing promotion, and so on.

JAVA ME

Java Platform Micro Edition (Java ME), formerly termed J2ME but still commonly referred to as such, is perhaps the most common platform for mobile application development today. Though somewhat riddled with marketing speak, the description from Java creator Sun Microsystems' website describes Java ME as follows:

> *"Java™ Platform, Micro Edition (Java ME) is the most ubiquitous application platform for mobile devices across the globe. It provides*

a robust, flexible environment for applications running on a broad range of other embedded devices, such as mobile phones, PDAs, TV set-top boxes, and printers.... Applications based on Java ME specifications are written once for a wide range of devices, yet exploit each device's native capabilities."

Because of this ubiquity, mobile developers have relied on Java ME for years, largely due to the number of devices that support the two platforms (rumored to be in the thousands). Developers also cite the learning curve as being relatively manageable compared to developing for other platforms, such as Symbian OS. A thorough resource for all things Java ME is Sun's **Java ME Reference section** (http://java.sun.com/javame/reference), which provides code samples, APIs, technical articles, and more. Also consider **J2ME Polish** (http://www.j2mepolish.org), an advanced build tool and GUI for Java ME applications.

Java ME is historically popular for mobile game development, yet many other types of productivity-related applications have been developed with it. Opera Mini, highlighted throughout this book, is a Java ME app. So is Google Maps Mobile (Figure 6-3).

Because Google Maps Mobile retrieves data from the web each time a request is made, it classifies as what is sometimes referred to as a **"smart client."** The term smart client refers to an application whose processing model lies somewhere between a "thin client" and "thick client." A thin client performs minimal to no client-side processing and data storage and then relies heavily on a central server for these two activities, whereas a thick client offers extensive client-side processing and data storage relatively independent of a central server. A simple example is the installation, processing and data storage differences between Microsoft Outlook (thick client) and Gmail (thin client).

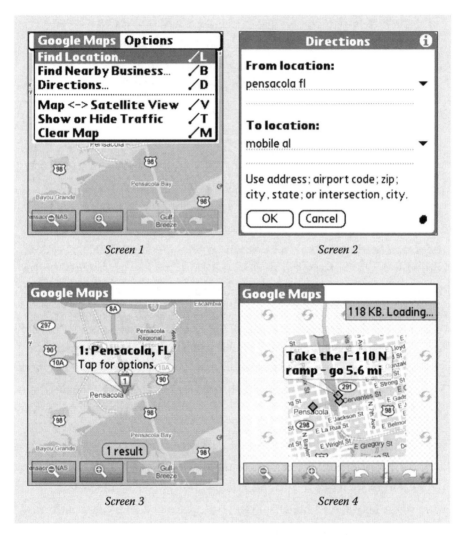

Figure 6-3. Google Maps Mobile (http://www.google.com/gmm), a Java ME application, installed on a Treo 650. User enters location (screens 1 and 2), receives search result (screen 3), and requests directions from first location to last location (screen 4).

A smart client, therefore, is a hybrid technology that offers a mixture of server-side and client-side computing. Typically smart clients require a fairly light client-side installation of software, offer basic client-side processing, and rely on server-side data storage and retrieval, though the mixture of client-side vs. server-side elements may vary from application to application.

Some of the advantages offered by smart clients over mobile browsing alone are evidenced in Figure 6-4, which shows user interface differences between using the Gmail smart client (left column) and Gmail accessed through a mobile browser (right column). First, greater visual control is extended to the designer for positioning elements, delineating messages, and organizing complex screen data. Second, application menus can be opened, closed, and overlaid within the viewable screen area, rather than embedding menu items at the top or bottom of a long, scrollable page. Third, developers can label and utilize a device's native **soft keys,** which are buttons located just below the screen that perform functions based on the screen label above the key, e.g. Options, Back, Close, etc.

Of the disadvantages of smart clients vs. mobile browsing, the most significant is the installation requirement. Mobile smart clients require software installation, which can be facilitated by visiting a web address provided by the content provider. However, the fact that a user must install software prior to consuming web content for each preferred content provider (e.g. Yahoo, BBC, ESPN) surfaces at least two problems: Users frequent dozens of content providers, and the software storage capacity of mobile devices is fairly limited. Imagine having to download a smart client for every website you would otherwise visit with a browser.

All things considered, Java ME and smart clients remain a viable option for serving and exchanging web content. Loyal users will often have no issues with downloading a smart client and may even prefer the user experience over browser-based interaction.

For additional reading, see **Thin and dumb, or fat and smart?** (http://www.w3.org/blog/MWITeam/2007/07/26/thin_and_dumb_or_fat_and_smart) by Dominique Hazael-Massieux, Activity Lead, W3C Mobile Web Initiative.

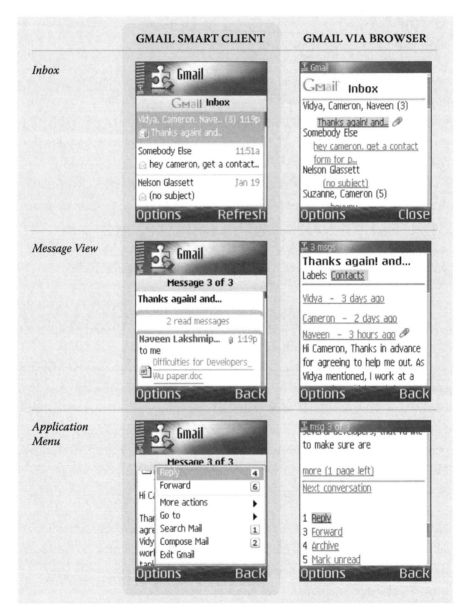

Figure 6-4. *User interface differences between the Gmail smart client (left) and Gmail accessed via browser (right). (Nokia 6680)*

SVG

SVG, or Scalable Vector Graphics, is "a language for describing two-dimensional graphics and graphical applications in XML."[3] Or in English, SVG enables a designer to render vector images and animations within the browser using numerical coordinates rather than pixels. SVG Tiny is a baseline profile of SVG, implementable on a range of devices, and described by the W3C thusly:

> *"In 2003, responding to industry demand and requests from the SVG developer community, the SVG Working Group introduced SVG Tiny, designed for mobile devices. SVG Tiny 1.1 provides an open standard solution for delivering graphical content that works equally well on handsets and desktops. SVG Tiny 1.2 introduces video, audio, gradients, stroke and fill opacity, styled text, and scripting capabilities into mobile devices."[4]*

SVG Tiny is supported, albeit inconsistently, by numerous mobile browsers including Opera Mobile, Access, Obigo, and one of the most globally available browsers, Openwave. Nokia's Series 60 platform has built-in support for SVG, and Flash Lite, discussed in the following section, currently supports SVG Tiny version 1.1, as do most Sony Ericsson phones model K700 and newer.[5] A full list of SVG-enabled devices can be found at http://svg.org/special/svg_phones.

An alternate but similar profile is SVG Basic, which was originally intended for higher-end devices such as PDAs, whereas SVG Tiny was intended for less-capable devices such as mobile phones. Notwithstanding, PDAs are becoming

---

[3] W3C, "Scalable Vector Graphics (SVG)," http://www.w3.org/Graphics/SVG.

[4] W3C Press Release, "World Wide Web Consortium Releases SVG Tiny 1.2 as a W3C Candidate Recommendation," August 10, 2006, http://www.w3.org/2006/08/svgtiny-pressrelease.

[5] Wikipedia, "Scalable Vector Graphics," http://en.wikipedia.org/wiki/Scalable_Vector_Graphics.

less common while mobile phones are becoming increasingly more capable, and it remains to be seen which of the two profiles will be preferred by developers.

Creating a basic SVG object isn't terribly complex, aside from understanding the mathematical attributes and values used to construct the object. But don't be dismayed if you're no Pythagoras—vector graphics programs such as Adobe Illustrator and Adobe Fireworks offer SVG export options, for SVG Tiny and SVG Basic profiles. For those who prefer to code by hand, below is a simple SVG Basic example lent by the good folks at Opera Software ASA, reprinted by permission (this code is also available at http://www.opera.com/products/desktop/svg).

```
 1. <?xml version="1.0" encoding="UTF-8"?>
 2. <!DOCTYPE svg PUBLIC "-//W3C//DTD SVG 1.1//EN"
 3.    "http://www.w3.org/Graphics/SVG/1.1/DTD/svg11-basic.dtd">
 4. <svg xmlns="http://www.w3.org/2000/svg" ↵
       xmlns:xlink="http://www.w3.org/1999/xlink">
 5.    <g fill-opacity="0.6" stroke="#fff" stroke-width="1px">
 6.       <circle cx="100px" cy="50px" r="50" fill="#00f" ↵
          transform="translate(0,0)" />
 7.       <circle cx="100px" cy="50px" r="50" fill="#ff0" ↵
          transform="translate(30,50)" />
 8.       <circle cx="100px" cy="50px" r="50" fill="#f0f" ↵
          transform="translate(-30,50)"/>
 9.    </g>
10. </svg>
```

Lines 2 and 3 are the DOCTYPE for SVG Basic.

Line 5 is the opening tag for the g **(or group) element,** which is a container element for grouping together related graphics elements.

Lines 6 through 8 plot three circles, establishing x and y coordinates, radius, fill color, and position. The rendered shapes appear as shown in Figure 6-5.

If the code example just shown were saved as **circles.svg**, the object (document) could be embedded in another HTML document using the `object` element, shown as follows:

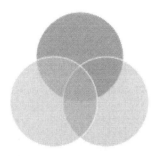

Figure 6-5. Three circles rendered as an SVG object.

```
<object data="/svg/circles.svg" width="220" height="150"></object>
```

For additional code examples, see W3Schools' **SVG Examples** available at http://www.w3schools.com/svg/svg_examples.asp. To view the examples on your desktop machine, you will need one of the following browsers: Firefox 2.x or newer, Safari 3.x or newer, Opera 9.x or newer.

FLASH LITE

Flash Lite is a lightweight version of the Adobe Flash Player developed specifically for mobile devices. Flash Lite 1.1, currently shipping on several devices from manufacturers including Nokia, Sony Ericsson, Samsung, and NTT DoCoMo, is based loosely on Flash 4 and therefore supports Flash 4 ActionScript. Flash 2.x, the most recent version at the time of writing, is based on Flash Player 7 and supports ActionScript 2.0. Flash 2.x works on multiple operating systems including Symbian and BREW.[6]

Flash Lite promises benefits akin to its desktop companion: Compatibility across platforms and visual consistency independent of the rendering engines. Additionally, "development time for applications is generally much shorter and cheaper with Flash Lite than Java ME," as asserted by Ryan Unger, Creative

---

[6] Adobe Flash Lite FAQ, http://www.adobe.com/products/flashlite/productinfo/faq/.

obile design agency Punchkick Interactive, in a recent interview by phone. Testing time is also generally shorter due to the inherent benefits of cross-platform compatibility and visual consistency. Lastly, Java ME and browser-based apps often fail to provide the rich content experiences afforded by Flash Lite, much like the Weather Channel prototype shown in Figure 6-6.

Figure 6-6. Flash Lite prototype app for The Weather Channel, viewed with a Samsung A950. (Image copyright Dave Yang. Used by permission.)

Drawbacks? Of course. But they all defer to one inescapable issue: Flash Lite, despite recent shipments on some newer devices, currently suffers from minimal market penetration. The number of Flash Lite installations on mobile devices is nowhere near the +95% penetration of Flash Player installations on PCs. For example, of the seven devices I own, only the Nokia 6680, a Series 60 device, offers Flash Lite support, and the installation had to be done manually. However, carriers and manufacturers alike are increasingly offering Flash-enabled devices. For example, Nokia already offers 56 handsets with Flash Lite pre-installed.[7] But until market penetration increases to a market majority or at least a significant minority, Flash Lite remains predominantly an early adopter technology with a promising future.

---

[7] Bill Perry, "56 Nokia Handsets Have Flash Lite Pre-Installed," http://www.flashdevices.net/2007/08/56-nokia-handsets-have-flash-lite-pre.html.

The amount of material required to provide a thorough introduction to Flash Lite development is too exhaustive for the purposes of this book, therefore the following resources are recommended.

- **Adobe Flash Lite product page** (with supporting development resources): http://www.adobe.com/products/flashlite
- *Foundation Flash Applications for Mobile Devices* by Weyert de Boer, Scott Janousek, and Richard Leggett: http://www.friendsofed.com/ book.html?isbn=1590595580
- **Nokia Flash Lite Visual Guide:** http://mobilewebbook.com/shorty/52666
- **Flash Devices** (a blog by Adobe manager Bill Perry): http:// www.flashdevices.net
- **NYC Traffic: Best Practices for Building Flash Lite Dynamic Content** (Adobe Developer Center): http://www.adobe.com/devnet/devices/articles/ dynamic_flashlite.html
- **"FlashLiteDev" Yahoo! Group:** http://tech.groups.yahoo.com/group/ FlashLite
- **Flash Lite Flickr Pool:** http://www.flickr.com/groups/flashlite/pool

LOCATION AWARENESS

Location awareness is just what it says—something being aware of its location. That something in a mobile sense is the device you hold in your hand. Often incorrectly referred to as **GPS** (Global Positioning System), location awareness is not necessarily a device or even a specific technology, such as GPS, but instead the *ability* for a device to know its location.

Tapping into the power of location produces the capacity to deliver extremely targeted, timely content. Services that utilize location-aware technology to do so are often referred to as **LBS,** which stands for Location-Based Services.

Recent research indicates a burgeoning demand for LBS in areas such as Europe, as reported by ZDNet.com contributor Alex Moskalyuk:

> *"Revenues from mobile location-based services (LBS) in the European market will grow by 34% annually to reach 622 mln euros in 2010, according to Berg Insight. Berg Insight forecasts that navigation will account for 48% of mobile LBS revenues in 2010. Berg Insight estimates that 18 mln mobile users in Europe will subscribe to location based billing plans by 2010."*[8]

In the U.S., because of the so-called "Wireless E911" mandate, carriers are required to aid 911 emergency dispatchers by providing the physical location of callers when an emergency call is placed. To comply with this mandate, some carriers ship handsets with GPS chips installed, while other carriers use a process called triangulation to locate a caller using nearby cell towers. Surprisingly, few carriers have opted to use these same mandated technologies to offer location-based services to customers, or for that matter, to make it possible for content providers to create LBS applications.

One carrier who has embraced location awareness is California-based **Helio,** an MVNO, or Mobile Virtual Network Operator, who leases mobile network service from Sprint Nextel. Helio equips its phones with GPS chips, but they don't stop there—Helio pre-installs a few location-aware applications on its GPS-enabled phones. One of these apps is Buddy Beacon (Figure 6-7). As described by Time Magazine reporter Anita Hamilton, "The new Drift phone from Helio comes with a feature called Buddy Beacon that lets you see your location on a map that pops up onscreen, thanks to the global positioning system (GPS) chip built into the phone. You can also see where any of your friends are—assuming that they authorize it and own the same $225 phone."[9]

---

[8] Alex Moskalyuk, "Location-Based Services in Europe to Grow at 34% a Year," http://blogs.zdnet.com/ITFacts/?p=11754.

[9] Anita Hamilton, "A Wireless Street Fight," http://www.time.com/time/magazine/article/0,9171,1590458,00.html.

Location awareness yields new opportunities to distribute, capture, and report data. "The mobile device has the potential to act as a significant reporter of data," says Ajit Jaokar, author of *Mobile Web 2.0*, "rather than a mere consumer of data."[10] Ajit classifies the types of data reported by mobile devices in three categories: **temporal** (time), **spatial** (location), and **personal** (ID, preferences, etc.). A practical combination of these three categories in one application is Yahoo!'s **ZoneTag** (http://zonetag.research.yahoo.com). Integrated with Flickr, ZoneTag is installed on a mobile phone and captures the temporal and spatial data of photos taken with the phone's camera. A user then uploads these photos to Flickr from her phone using ZoneTag, and all three data classes— time stamp, tags (including location), Flickr ID—are reported to Flickr, which

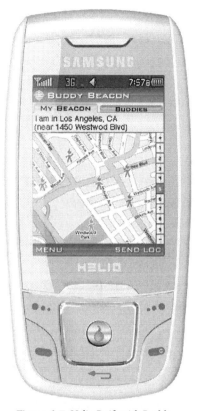

Figure 6-7. Helio Drift with Buddy Beacon installed. (Image copyright Helio, LLC. Used by permission.)

creates a page to display the photo with the accompanying meta data. Sample ZoneTag photos can be seen at http://www.flickr.com/photos/tags/zonetag/ interesting.

Another example, albeit somewhat hypothetical but much discussed nonetheless, combines texting with location awareness to deliver automated

---

[10] Ajit Jaokar, "Mobile Web 2.0: Web 2.0 and Its Impact On the Mobility and Digital Convergence," http://opengardensblog.futuretext.com/archives/2005/12/ mobile_web_20_w.html

messages to subscribed users whenever they come within a specified distance from a store or other physical location. In theory, this could result in a Londoner receiving opt-in, automated text messages about promotions, discounts, or new items according to pre-established preferences as he passes his favorite store on foot or in car. Obviously, the potential for abuse by marketers is of great concern. Imagine the oft-cited example of receiving a text message every time you passed a Starbucks—nearly every block in some major U.S. cities!

However, the possibility of delivering targeted, timely content using location-aware applications remains within reach, either immediately or in the near future. We've barely scratched the surface when it comes to thinking about ways to leverage location awareness. Although the concept has yet to reach that elusive tipping point and some argue it never will (see http://www.russellbeattie.com/blog/my-thoughts-on-consumer-lbs), others, including myself, expect it to within the next couple years.

WIDGETS

In recent years, widgets have been widely popularized due to the success of **Yahoo! Widgets** and **Mac OS X Dashboard.** Widget, a term that traditionally refers to operating system GUI components such as dialog boxes or pop-up windows, is also used to describe small, lightweight applications that run within a local client. These "micro" applications are very compact in both physical size and file size and usually perform only one or two simple functions.

Widgets are meant to be a transient, quick experience for the user, as compared to the sovereign, in-depth experience of full-scale applications. They run alongside other widgets, allowing users to quickly switch between the lot and add or delete widgets at their discretion. Because of these attributes, the applicability for mobile usage is a logical fit, specifically widgets created to interact with web content. The absence of tabbed browsing, easy switching between applications, and broadband network speeds gives rise to the need for a dashboard-like assortment of small, quick, customizable apps. Widgets are one of the ways to fill this need.

For the developer, the blend of technology required to create a widget is a familiar mix: XHTML, CSS, and JavaScript. A widget is usually fed fresh content via API or RSS feed (see section that follows) from an existing content source, but they can also be fed completely custom content created specifically for the widget. Several content providers, software vendors, and even manufacturers offer the necessary software to display widgets on mobile devices. Some of these include **Bluepulse** (http://www.bluepulse.com), **Moblets** (http://mojax.mfoundry.com/display/mojax/Moblets), and Nokia's **WidSets** (http://www.widsets.com).

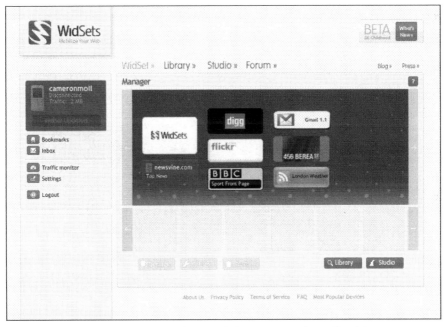

Figure 6-8. Nokia Widsets are managed from a desktop PC using the WidSets Manager.

WidSets are cross-platform widgets that can be used on devices from a wide variety manufacturers, in addition to Nokia devices. Some widgets have been created by Nokia, while the larger, remaining share have been created by the WidSets community. A brief overview for creating your own WidSets widget can be found here: http://ajaxian.com/archives/widsets-nokia-mobile-widgets.

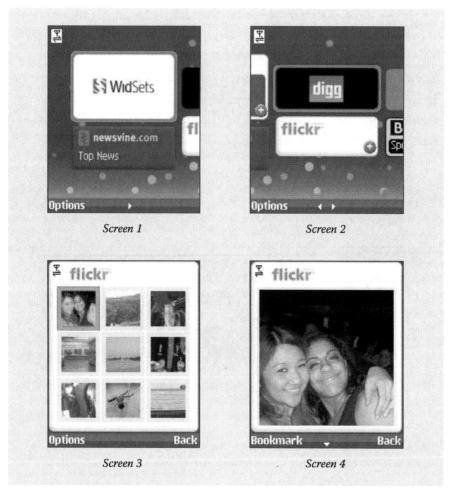

Figure 6-9. Once a user has selected his or her widgets of choice using the WidSets Manager, those widgets are transferred to the user's mobile device.

The management of WidSets widgets takes place on a desktop PC. A user customizes his choice of the number and placement of widgets (Figure 6-8). Once these settings have been saved, the widget arrangement is transferred to the user's mobile device (Figure 6-9).

The process is admittedly less than ideal, given it would be preferable to manage and utilize widgets without relying on a PC. But you can likely expect future versions of WidSets and other widget software packages to offer widget management entirely within the mobile environment.

For additional reading, see **Mobile Widgets: The Ubiquitous Mobile Web** (http://www.pavingways.com/mobile-widgets-the-ubiquitous-mobile-web_84.html) by Rocco Georgi, as well as Mahalo's **Mobile Widgets** directory page located at http://www.mahalo.com/Mobile_Widgets.

RSS & APIs

RSS feeds and APIs form the foundation for much of the content shared on the web today. The portability and exchange of data provided by these two technologies is at the heart of that oh-so-trendy buzzword "Web 2.0"—the shift from organization-created content to user-created content, the web treated as a platform, the development frenzy of "mashups," and so on.

RSS, short for Really Simple Syndication, is an XML-based format for sharing and delivering regularly updated web content, such as news, blog posts, and notifications. Output files are referred to as RSS feeds, and these feeds can be read using feed reader or RSS aggregator software. RSS feeds can also be used to embed, aggregate, or republish content in other websites and applications.

API, or Application Program Interface, is essentially a way to communicate with a content provider's database in XML format. Like RSS, APIs can be used to embed, aggregate, or republish content in other websites and applications. However, unlike RSS, the capabilities offered by an API allow a developer to repurpose the content in ways not afforded by RSS alone. "By exposing the inner workings of their site or application via an API, the site provider allows the community to make of it what they will," says Gareth Rushgrove in his API primer, **APIs and Mashups For The Rest Of Us** (http://www.digital-web.com/ articles/apis_and_mashups). "Applications can be extended in ways that may have been impossible, uneconomical, or unimaginable for the original developers to do themselves."

The beauty of these two technologies is that they can be utilized and even combined to present optimized content to mobile users. Sites such as **LiteFeeds** (http://www.litefeeds.com) and **Feed2Mobile** (http:// feed2mobile.kaywa.com) offer mobile-friendly feed reading and feed creation, respectively. But a far more stunning example of RSS/API integration is **Leaflets** (http://getleaflets.com). Developed by Seattle-based Blue Flavor, Leaflets use RSS feeds and APIs to present mobile versions of popular web content, such as Flickr, del.icio.us, and Newsvine (Figure 6-10).

Optimized for iPhone[11], Leaflets offer a rich web experience created entirely using RSS feeds and APIs, polished with a few advanced CSS properties such as multiple background images in a single element. Those sites that offer only RSS, such as Newsvine, are displayed with an interface similar to a feed reader, whereas those that offer greater access to and manipulation of content via API, such as Flickr, function much like a mini web app.

Because of the cross-platform, cross-browser, cross-device, cross-just-about-everything nature of XML content, RSS and API are two technologies worth strongly considering when developing mobile web content.

---

[11] It's fair to state at this convenient juncture in time that I don't recommend creating content optimized for a single device, iPhone or any other, but instead I encourage creating content optimized for the mobile experience. Alas, if it makes good business sense for you to optimize for a single device, who am I to rain on your party?

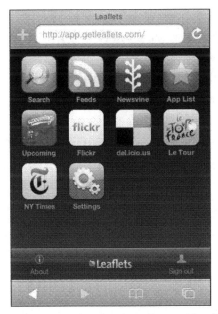 

Figure 6-10. Blue Flavor's Leaflets, a widget-like collection of RSS- and API-based web content. (Apple iPhone)

AJAX

As the two terms are often improperly interchanged, let's clarify the difference between JavaScript and Ajax. **JavaScript** is a scripting language used to enhance or modify the presentation layer of a page by interacting with HTML source code, typically at the client-side rather than server-side level.

Ajax (or AJAX), a term coined by Jesse James Garrett that means Asynchronous Javascript and XML, refers not to a scripting language but rather to a method for creating rich web interaction. JavaScript is one of the languages used to create this interaction, XML is the other (though HTML can also be used). The two work to manipulate the Document Object Model (DOM). But it is the asynchronous part that has ignited the use of Ajax in many web applications.

With Ajax, small trips are made to the server in the background (usually via a generic API called XMLHttpRequest) as the user interacts with a page, without having to reload the entire page every time data is requested. This is what asynchronous refers to—server communication that is not synchronous with page reloading. Asynchronous server communication reduces the amount of data transferred and increases the responsiveness of an application, and these benefits warrant merit for the mobile web, as the traditional click-refresh, click-refresh browsing experience can be painfully slow on a mobile device.

Ajax—already supported by Opera Mobile, Opera Mini 4.0 beta, Nokia/Symbian (WebKit-based versions), Pocket IE, and MobileSafari—has the potential to vastly improve the mobile web experience. Ajit Jaokar believes it will, and has even argued that Ajax "will be the preferred platform of choice for mobile applications at the expense of Java ME and XHTML."[12] Additionally, because Ajax is a method and not a language or platform, any mobile browser that supports JavaScript and XMLHttpRequest is a probable candidate for Ajax support.

However, as with many of the technologies mentioned in this book, Ajax has its fair share of drawbacks. The first, of course, is compatibility. Ajax simply isn't supported by the larger part of devices in the market today, making it a viable option usually only for higher-end devices. Second, scripting and continuous server connections tend to increase processor activity and therefore increase battery consumption. As strange as it sounds, Ajax can actually drain a handset's battery rather quickly. Lastly, because Ajax requires many small trips to the server instead of just a few large trips per usage, intermittence and slower networks can produce latency issues. As Andy Moore quipped in a recent email conversation, "There are enough badly

---

[12] Ajit Jaokar, "AJAX for Mobile Devices Will Be the Hallmark of 'Mobile Web 2.0' in 2006," http://wbt.sys-con.com/read/167026.htm.

written, browser-crashing Ajax apps on the desktop web without XMLHttpRequest creeping its way into the mobile realm."

Drawbacks aside, it's certainly possible to begin utilizing Ajax immediately. **37signals,** developers of web-based applications such as Basecamp and Backpack, recently deployed an iPhone-optimized version of their to-do list app, **Ta-da List** (http://

Figure 6-11. iPhone-optimized version of Ta-da List, developed by 37signals. (Image copyright 37signals, LLC. Used by permission.)

www.tadalist.com). The interface is rich with Ajax interaction, enabling the user to add, edit, and delete list items within a single page (Figure 6-11).

Others, such as Rocco Georgi, Lead Developer of PavingWays, have been not only discussing but also demonstrating possibilities for mobile Ajax implementation since early 2006. Rocco, a pragmatic optimist, offers a number of resources for mobile Ajax, including an overview page (http://www.pavingways.com/mobile-ajax), Frost Ajax library (http://www.pavingways.com/frost-ajax-library), YouTube video (http://youtube.com/watch?v=GIeAisUYcLk), and working examples such as an event finder application (http://www.pavingways.com/mobile-ajax-application-test-and-demo_69.html), about which he writes the following:

> *"[C]ross-platform Mobile AJAX really is possible, because already many mobile web browsers support the XMLHttpRequest [XHR]. For those that do not support it, the application needs to provide fall-backs, so it works without XHR as well. The event finder demo*

accordingly works on different mobile browsers: Pocket IE (IE Mobile), Opera Mobile (not Mini) and even Minimo [Mozilla] make use of the AJAX capabilities, while other browsers, such as Opera Mini still work and just reload the whole page everytime you click somewhere."

For additional reading, see **Mobile Ajax Today** (http:// weblog.cenriqueortiz.com/index.php/Mobility/2006/10/17/Mobile-AJAX-Today) by C. Enrique Ortiz. There are also plenty of Ajax **introductions** and **tutorials** available on the web, but for all things Ajax, few resources are as complete and current as **Ajaxian.com.**

IN DEFENSE OF THE BROWSER

The technologies mentioned in this chapter beg the question, Is the browser model a flawed approach for mobile? Does it encourage miniaturization of content, given the current inconsistencies of markup rendering and the deficiencies of carrier networks? Should we look entirely beyond the browser and leverage only technologies created specifically for mobile devices?

Short answer? No. The success of the web, as we know it today, is largely due to one piece of software: **the browser.** I can access nearly any website, application (including email), or other forms of content with that one browser. To assume users will be satisfied downloading a smart client or widget for every site they frequent, or for every content provider they associate themselves with, is to assume users have adequate storage space on their devices and that they are willing to pay the costs, both data and time, to download these content-provider applications. For every argument against the browser, there's likely a case study demonstrating devices and networks specific to a content-provider are rarely successful.[13] In all likelihood, most

---

[13] See "Merill Lynch: Time to Pull Plug on Mobile ESPN," http://www.mediaweek.com/mw/news/recent_display.jsp?vnu_content_id=1002876073.

users will probably download a smart client or widget for a couple of their favorite content providers, but beyond that a browser will be—or should be—sufficient for interacting with web content.

PROMOTING YOUR CONTENT

YOU'VE ARRIVED. YOU'VE EXPLORED ALL YOUR options, mobilized your content, developed, tested, and validated. Now how about rewarding yourself by shuttling users to your shiny new masterpiece? The following resources will aid you in promoting your content.

.MOBI

In October 2006, ".mobi," a top-level domain (TLD) created specifically for mobile websites, was made available for registration by the general public. The effort of bringing this new TLD to market was years in the making and backed by mobile giants such as Ericsson, Nokia, Samsung, T-Mobile, Vodafone, and others. To date more than 500,000 .mobi names have been registered.[1]

Its introduction wasn't without considerable debate from the mobile community. Some developers, such as Russell Beattie, formerly of Yahoo! Mobile, argued a new TLD was precisely what was needed to kick-start the mobile web (http://www.russellbeattie.com/notebook/1008931.html):

> *"Now users can guess 'cnn.mobi' or 'yahoo.mobi' or 'amazon.mobi' and KNOW that their phone isn't going to barf at them, and the companies will have a standard name to rally around as well....*

---

[1] MobileMonday Global, "Ferrari and Rolls-Royce Do dotMobi," May 2, 2007, http://www.mobilemonday.net/news/ferrari-and-rolls-royce-do-dotmobi.

Unlike TLDs like .info, .biz, .pro, or .name, .mobi solves a real problem that people have today and will still have tomorrow."

Others, such as Carlo Longino of MobHappy.com, questioned whether an alternate domain was even necessary, asserting it was a frivolous replacement for device detection, a technique that's already been in use for several years (http://mobhappy.com/blog1/2006/05/23/mobi-kickstarting-the-mobile-web-or-holding-it-back):

> *"The biggest risk is that site owners will buy a .mobi domain, throw up an XHTML-MP site, and leave it at that, thinking they've got this mobile thing sorted out—after all, they've got a site using .mobi, that thing that's supposed to make the mobile Web happen.... [This approach is] more exclusionary than exclusive, leaving the hard work up to the end user, when it could better be done on the [server] side of the site."*

In reality, both sides of the issue warrant merit. On the one hand, utilizing a secondary domain (a four-character TLD, no less) just for mobile content can be a challenge for users to remember or even type. On the other hand, chances are you'll need a secondary domain of some sort anyway—even if using device detection—to store mobile-specific files, whether a simple directory, a sub-domain, or an entirely new domain. At the very least, .mobi provides a unified convention for naming the location of these files.

While the debate still continues, .mobi domain names continue to be registered in large numbers. Should you decide to follow suit, the following resources may be useful:

- **.mobi registrars:** http://pc.mtld.mobi/switched/findaregistrar.html
- **.mobi website showcase:** http://showcase.mtld.mobi

WAP PUSH

"WAP Push" is a term used to describe the process of requesting and accessing a web address by text message. Given the ubiquity of texting, combined with the difficulty of data entry on mobile devices, WAP Push is a relatively simple solution to the problem of typing a lengthy web address on a numeric keypad. Users can text a very brief message via SMS and then receive a reply with a link in the message. Clicking this link will open the device's native browser and send the user to a specified location. This enables content providers to send users directly to content deep within a site, while masking the lengthy web address behind that content.

To understand the benefit of WAP Push for users, consider the example from **FeedBurner** shown in Figure 7-1, which relies on traditional web address entry:

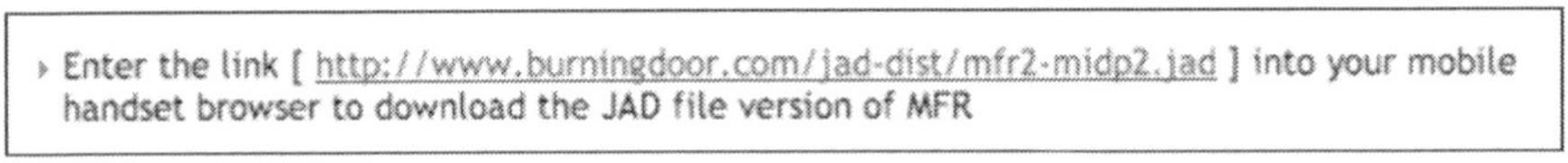

> ‣ Enter the link [http://www.burningdoor.com/jad-dist/mfr2-midp2.jad] into your mobile handset browser to download the JAD file version of MFR

Figure 7-1. A less-effective example of entering a URL on your mobile handset.

Type that web address using my handset's numeric keypad? Download the "JAD"? No wonder some fear using the web on their mobile if they have to "download the JAD" by multi-tapping 50 characters.[2]

Contrast that with the example shown in Figure 7-2, which uses WAP Push. Text the message "SHOT" to Short Code 84118 and you'll receive a reply with a link to web content. Easy peasy. (Note: This short code will work only in the region where the advertisement appeared, probably somewhere in Europe where WAP Push is prevalent).

---

[2] Domainatron (http://pukupi.com/tools/domainatron) is a tool that calculates the number of keystrokes required to type a web address on a typical i-mode (Japan) mobile. Typing the URL in the FeedBurner example would require more than 100 keystrokes!

For additional WAP Push reading, see **WAP Push Services** (http://www.palowireless.com/wap/wappush.asp) for WAP Push overviews, tutorials, and resources, as well as Adam Bird's tutorial **Create WAP Push SMS Messages** (http://www.codeproject.com/cs/internet/wappush.asp).

Figure 7-2. Sony Ericsson advertisement with WAP Push instructions.

MATRIX CODES

As evidenced with WAP Push, entering a lengthy URL using a numeric keypad, even a QWERTY keypad, can be a frustrating experience at best. Another solution that aims to facilitate URL entry and targeted content delivery is a technology consisting of black and white patterns that encode text or raw data. Referred to as data matrix codes, these two-dimensional barcodes function much like traditional vertical-line barcodes but can encode much more data (up to 2,335 alphanumeric characters).[3]

In recent years, software developers have discovered ways to utilize matrix codes in conjunction with mobile phones, specifically camera-equipped models. Two emerging standards are **QR codes** (mainly Asia) and **Semacodes** (North America).

---

[3] Wikipedia, "Data Matrix," http://en.wikipedia.org/wiki/Data_Matrix.

Wikipedia describes the creation and use of Semacodes pertaining to web content as follows:

> *"Using Semacode SDK software, a URL can be converted into a type of barcode resembling a crossword puzzle, which is called a 'tag'. Tags can be quickly captured with a mobile phone's camera and decoded to obtain a Web site address. This address can then be accessed via the phone's web browser."*

QR codes work much the same as Semacodes. In fact, with the proper software installed on your handset, you can use the Wikipedia QR code in Figure 7-3 to go directly to http:// en.wikipedia.org merely by taking a picture of the code on this page using your handset's camera.

Figure 7-3. The QR code for the Wikipedia home page (English version).

As for drawbacks to this approach, there are a few. Users must have a camera-equipped handset, and they must install software that recognizes matrix codes. Content providers must embed their codes in print or screen material advertising their products or services and hope that users with the appropriate handset/software combination encounter these codes.

Additional resources:

- **Semacode Official Site:** http://semacode.org
- **Semapedia** (Wikipedia + Semacodes): http://www.semapedia.org
- **QR Codes in America?** by Kelly Goto: http://www.gotomobile.com/ archives/qr-codes-in-america

- **The Mobile Codeatron** (QR code generator): http://pukupi.com/tools/codeatron
- **Kaywa QR Code Generator:** http://qrcode.kaywa.com
- **Direct Access to Mobile Web Content Sans URIs** by Cameron Moll: http://www.cameronmoll.com/archives/001191.html

MOBILE ADVERTISING

While often considered a nuisance by consumers, advertising is largely responsible for funding the operations of today's most popular websites: Google, Yahoo, MSN, and many more. You might be annoyed by their ads, but you endure them nonetheless to gain access to their useful applications and services. And you might even click them once in a while.

Mobile advertising has been gaining considerable traction in recent years, but not without skepticism, as reported by Forrester Research:

> *"Although 79 percent of consumers find the idea of mobile ads annoying, early efforts at mobile marketing have revealed that consumers will happily engage in campaigns as long as marketers deliver valuable information or content.... To combat preconditioned skepticism, marketers must recognize that mobile marketing is about offering value, not interrupting consumers with unmoving and irrelevant ads."*[4]

The mobile advertising industry, which includes text message ads, mobile TV ads, website ads, and games and music ads, churned through $871 million in paid services during 2006 (Figure 7-4). Text message ads dominated advertising budgets, while mobile website ads trailed a very distant third.

---

[4] Forrester Research, "US Consumers Are Ready For Mobile Marketing," January 4, 2007, http://phx.corporate-ir.net/phoenix.zhtml?c=60569&p=irol-newsArticle&ID=946640.

TYPE	SPEND
Text Message Ads	$629 million
Mobile TV Ads	$173 million
Mobile Website Ads	$36 million
Mobile Games & Music Ads	$34 million
2006 Total (Global)	**$871 million**

Figure 7-4. Global advertising expenditures by ad type in 2006.[5] (Total isn't exact due to rounding.)

However, mobile website ads may soon begin to shed some of the distance behind text message ads. Japanese mobile operator NTT DoCoMo Inc. has been posting small banner ads—not unlike those shown in Figure 7-5—on mobile sites since 2000. They report displaying 1.5 billion ads to subscribers in 2006.

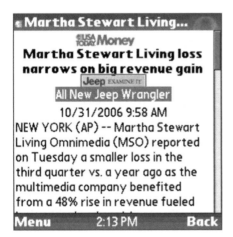

Figure 7-5. Left: Banner ad for Jeep Wrangler on USA Today Mobile, http://wap.usatoday.com. (Treo 650, Opera Mini) Right: Banner ad for Windows Mobile on The New York Times Mobile, http://mobile.nytimes.com. (Sony Ericsson, NetFront browser)

---

[5] Amol Sharma, "Companies Vie for Ad Dollars on Mobile Web," Wall Street Journal, Jan 17, 2007.

In Fall 2006, Google entered the mobile ad space by expanding its AdWords service to include mobile ads. Figure 7-6 shows one of these ads inserted above search results, the same as you've seen atop desktop search results.

The web advertising industry is replete with best practices and guidelines, and mobile is no exception. The **Mobile Marketing Association** (MMA, http://mmaglobal.com) is currently the accepted body for governing mobile

Figure 7-6. Text ad for Royal Discount inserted above Google search results. (Treo 650, Opera Mini)

marketing. They've released a number of recommendations for ad sizes, ethics, etc. (Figure 7-7) available here: http://mmaglobal.com/modules/content/index.php?id=118.

Barbara Ballard discusses various ad types (banner, interstitial, fisheye) in her book, *Designing the Mobile User Experience,* and advertising excerpts from the book can be found here: http://mobilewebbook.com/shorty/23794. Lastly, don't pass up the comprehensive article from dotMobi, **Mobile Advertising: How to Monetize Your Mobile Site** (http://dev.mobi/node/422).

Click-through Capabilities Guidelines		
Landing Page Type	Technical Guidelines	Sample Creative

Standard	• **Header Image:**
	  - 112 x 20 pixels
	  - 16 color gif
	• **Text for Jump Page:**
	  - 6 lines of text appear before user scrolls
	  - 32 characters per line (including spaces)	

Email Opt-in	• **Header Image:**
	  - 112 x 20 pixels
	  - 16 color gif
	• **Text for Jump Page:**
	  - 6 lines of text appear before user scrolls
	  - 32 characters per line (including spaces)
	• **Email Opt-in:**
	  - Enter e-mail address for more information
	  - E-mail should include link for consumers to opt-out	

Click-to-Call	• **Header Image:**
	  - 112 x 20 pixels
	  - 16 color gif
	• **Text for Jump Page:**
	  - 6 lines of text appear before user scrolls
	  - 32 characters per line (including spaces)
	• **Click-to-Call:**
	  - Phone number for users to call
	  - Preferably specific number to track campaign	

Figure 7-7. MMA Mobile Advertising Guidelines, fourth revision (http://www.mmaglobal.com/ mobileadvertising.pdf).

TOWARDS A DESIRABLE MOBILE WEB

AROUND THE TIME I BEGAN AUTHORING *Mobile Web Design* I boarded a flight to Portland and pulled out another book that had been in my possession for a couple months, given as a gift while in London speaking at @MEDIA 2006 on the same topic you're reading about. *Never Push When It Says Pull* is a book of "small rules for little problems." Or so the token book says. I couldn't get through half of it, let alone the first few pages, without a good chuckle every now and then.

About an hour into the flight I stumbled on the following from the segment, "How to write a novel":

> "*Before you start you need to decide how fat your book is going to be. ... Short books have sad endings because in order to have a happy ending you have to start happy, get sad and then regain happiness. Short books don't have time for all this, so they start miserable and get worse quickly.*"

Yikes, I hope that hasn't been the case with this book! Short? Yes. Miserable? I certainly hope not. In fact, the mobile web is a fascinating subject, and there are plenty of happy endings to be had by embracing it.

Yet these happy endings won't come by happenstance. There's a good chance you've already accessed web content on your mobile device prior to reading this book. And there's an even better chance you were not delighted by the experience. This disconnect between the desire to consume content and the ensuing experience highlights the need for mobile web experiences that are desirable, dependable, and disciplined. *Desirable* in that the overall experience is usable, affordable, and contextual. *Dependable* in that we can expect greater consistency across devices, a more standardized markup language, and increased usage convention among mobile sites and applications. And *disciplined* in that the content provided is relevant to the limitations and opportunities of being mobile.

The production of desirable mobile user experiences will require the combined efforts of device manufacturers, browser developers, content providers, and ultimately you. Mobile consumers will implore you to create, devise, and develop mobile-compatible content. The mobile industry needs your experience. Your talent. Your innate ability to solve problems users are facing while being mobile. Your vision for creating unforeseen opportunities within the mobile space. And your voice to encourage your organization and others to mobilize their web content.

So, what are you waiting for? Put down this book and get started already!

ABOUT CAMERON MOLL

Co-author of *CSS Mastery* and author of *Mobile Web Design*, Cameron Moll creates meaningful web interfaces that harmonize utility and presentation. His work or advice has been featured by Forrester Research, Communication Arts, National Public Radio (NPR), HOW Magazine, .net Magazine, and many others. He speaks on user interface design at conferences nationally and internationally, and amid all this craziness he still finds time to play ball with each of his boys.

He also manages AuthenticJobs.com, a targeted destination for standards-aware designers and developers and the companies seeking to hire them.

Cameron is currently employed as Principal Interaction Designer for the LDS Church, helping to create and manage the many websites and applications of a organization with more than 12 million members worldwide. Cameron resides in Salt Lake City, Utah with his wife Suzanne and four sons. Find him online at http://cameronmoll.com.